Beyond Storybooks:

Young Children and the Shared Book Experience

Judith Pollard Slaughter
McGill University

 International Reading Association
Newark, Delaware 19714

The International Reading Association attempts, through its publications, to provide a forum for a wide spectrum of opinions on reading. This policy permits divergent viewpoints without assuming the endorsement of the Association.

Director of Publications Joan M. Irwin
Managing Editor Romayne McElhaney
Associate Editor Anne Fullerton
Associate Editor Karen Goldsmith
Assistant Editor Amy Trefsger
Production Department Manager Iona Sauscermen
Graphic Design Coordinator Boni Nash
Mechanical Preparation Cheryl Strum
Design Consultant Larry Husfelt
Typesetting Systems Analyst Wendy Mazur
Typesetting Anette Schuetz-Ruff
                 Richard James
Proofing Florence Pratt

Library of Congress Cataloging in Publication Data

Slaughter, Judith Pollard, 1938–
    Beyond storybooks: Young children and the shared book experience/Judith Pollard Slaughter.
        p.   cm.
    Includes bibliographical references (p.   ) and indexes.
    1. Reading (Primary)—Language experience approach.   2. English language—
Composition and exercises—Study and teaching (Primary).   3. Children—Books and reading.   I. Title.
LB1525.34.S56   1992   92-32773
372.4'14—dc20   CIP
ISBN 0-87207-377-7

Contents

On Gaining a Literate Identity

Dorothy Menosky, an early advocate of whole language, tells this story of an encounter with a four-year-old girl she met on a recent trip to Hawaii.

The little girl was reading some version of *Little Red Riding Hood*. "Oh, I see you're reading *Little Red Riding Hood*," Dorothy said.

"I'm not *reading* it," the little girl responded rather emphatically. "I'm just looking at the pictures. I'll learn to read when I'm in kindergarten."

"Oh, I thought you were reading," Dorothy said.

"Well, I wasn't. I can't read."

Dorothy's trip proceeded and so did the little girl and her reading. Dorothy saw her again later on, and the little girl now was actually mouthing some of the words in the text. "I thought you couldn't read," Dorothy whispered to the little girl.

"I wasn't reading! I was just remembering," the little girl said.

Later Dorothy caught the little girl turning back a page to look more carefully at the text, after which she turned the page and maintained her focus on the text rather than on the pictures. "I caught you," Dorothy said. "You were too reading."

"Okay!" the little girl said, somewhat exasperated. "So probably I did read just that one little part!"

We like this language story because it illustrates that the major task we face as reading teachers of young children is helping those children *identify* themselves as readers. Children come to school already reading. They can read stop signs and the brand name on the toothpaste tube; they can spot a McDonald's from up to three miles away. Our task is not to teach them to read per se, but to identify what it is they can read and support them in the process of making other print familiar and understandable.

Judith Slaughter argues that one easy way to begin is with predictable books. What child can't read Martin's *Brown Bear, Brown Bear* or Goss and Harste's *It Didn't Frighten Me!* after they are introduced through a shared book experience? When we and Lynn Rhodes coined the term "predictable books,"

little did we know how popular a term it was going to become. We wanted simply to give a name to those books that made access to reading easy for children. Predictable books have texts children quickly become comfortable with, texts that meet these five criteria:

1. The pictures support the text.

2. Large chunks of language are repeated so that one page often cues the reader as to what will be found on the next.

3. The language used is literary but natural, often sounding like oral language.

4. The story line reflects things that happen in the real world—that is, rabbits hop down holes, snakes slither in the grass, and so on.

5. The language is chunked in such a fashion that it has a cadence or rhythm that supports the reading of the text.

Lynn Rhodes took it upon herself to organize the first list of predictable books; this book extends that sort of simple resource by suggesting many activities related to sharing predictable books that teachers can use in their classrooms on a daily basis. These activities are organized around the shared book experience, an approach that attempts to duplicate the bedtime story or "lap reading" experiences many children have prior to coming to school. Predictable books are often put in Big Book format so a group of children can see the text as they participate in its being read aloud. As an instructional technique, shared reading helps children develop mental expectations about new print settings and supports them in seeing as predictable, comprehensible, and *readable* an ever-greater variety of print.

Early childhood educators, special education teachers, and others who work with students who are new—and even those who are more seasoned—to literacy will find Judith Slaughter's *Beyond Storybooks* invaluable. It demonstrates how teachers can use predictable books and the shared book experience as a resource for reading and writing, as well as for inquiry across the curriculum. As such it will inspire creative teachers and children to come up with thousands of extensions of their own, once they get the hang of it and realize the many possibilities. In the process, they will become curriculum planners and developers and will take ownership of their own teaching and learning.

Jane Decker, a first grade teacher from Columbia, Missouri, always begins her school year with one of her favorite predictable books, a story about a sick little boy who must stay in bed and misses out on lots of exciting things going on in his neighborhood. Before sharing the story, Jane encourages the children to use their background experiences and to look closely at the pictures to see if they can predict why the boy is in bed. The first graders crowd around and one of them invariably notices that the child has spots all over his face; often someone else suggests that the boy has measles or chickenpox. The children then discuss a number of things that might happen in the story. But one year, things began differently. The children in that class crowded around the book as usual, but when it came to predicting, Nathan, who had obviously kept up on changes in his world, sucked in his breath and offered, "I bet he's got herpes!"

Just as each reading of a predictable book holds new possibilities for Jane Decker and her students, so literacy and literacy instruction will never be the same once you discover the joys of predictable books and the shared book experience through reading this volume.

Happy literacy to all, and to all the identity of being literate.

Jerome C. Harste
Carolyn L. Burke
Indiana University

INTRODUCTION

In recent years, educators have learned a great deal about emergent literacy by observing young children as they acquire and use language naturally. Educators have come to realize that a child's early environment has an enormous impact on language development. If, for example, children live in homes where literature and reading are valued, where bedtime stories are a treasured part of the day, and where they are encouraged to draw and print, they have a distinct advantage in learning to read and write. This knowledge has begun to influence pedagogical practice. Teachers of young children are now being encouraged to create supportive environments and to use a variety of techniques to assist all children in extending what they already know about language.

The procedures and activities described in this book center on the idea of helping children learn to read through the "shared book experience." The essential tools for this approach are predictable stories, often in Big Book format, that can be shared with an entire class by a teacher who models the act of reading. These read-aloud sessions can lead into concrete learning experiences that help children build on what they know about print to become more proficient language users. Children enjoy hearing the predictable stories on which these activities are based, and their enthusiasm translates into a desire to know more about the language and meaning of print. This general approach can form the basis of all literacy teaching in the early childhood classroom, or it can be used in conjunction with other programs designed to teach emergent literacy, such as one of the many commercial reading/language arts series.

Beyond Storybooks is intended primarily for teachers and others who work with children from approximately three to eight years of age; the information provided here will also be of interest to parents, librarians, school administrators, and students of education. The suggested activities are geared toward children who are just beginning to acquire literacy (emergent readers) and new readers who are maturing in their literacy abilities (developing readers). Teach-

ers of slightly older children who are experiencing difficulty in learning to read and write (at-risk readers) should also find the ideas and information in this book helpful.

Chapter 1 provides an overview of the way children acquire literacy and describes in more detail the shared book experience, predictable literature, and practices appropriate for teaching young children. Chapter 2 describes the materials needed to implement the shared book experience and offers suggestions for introducing books in the classroom. Specific activities designed to promote the acquisition and development of literacy are provided in Chapter 3. Writing activities are the focus of Chapter 4, while Chapter 5 shows how the shared book experience can be integrated across the curriculum. Chapter 6 describes two specific theme units and in this context explores ideas for managing the classroom, keeping records, and evaluating students' progress. Finally, the appendix describes approximately 120 widely available predictable storybooks in an annotated bibliography and lists a number of other resources.

The ability to read and write is one of the most important gifts any teacher or parent can give to a child. I believe that the shared book experience is the best approach for helping young children become skilled readers and writers. Children will acquire positive attitudes about books and reading and develop a confidence that will enrich their learning in the early grades—and beyond.

JPS
Montreal, Canada

CHAPTER ONE

Why the Shared Book Experience?

Many children know a great deal about print and books before they receive any formal instruction. Their parents and others read stories to them, and children imitate this behavior by going through favorite books on their own and "reading" them from memory, often with amazing accuracy (Doake, 1985). Children see advertisements on television and begin to associate products with printed brand names; they see traffic and commercial shop signs and learn about print in their environment. Information about letters and sounds is presented in countless ways in daily life, and children are quick to pick up on this information. Even very young children invent or duplicate sounds and letters in an attempt to communicate messages of their own.

In recent years, educators have learned an enormous amount about the early stages of literacy development by observing young children as they acquire and use language naturally. Durkin (1966, 1974), Jackson (1988), Pinsent (1988), and Torrey (1979), for example, have conducted studies of children who learned to read before entering school. These children were curious and excited about books and words. Their parents supported their interest by providing them with things such as storybooks, chalkboards and chalk, paper, crayons, and pencils. And when these children were very young, their parents and others frequently read stories aloud to them.

In addition to paving the way for literacy learning, reading stories aloud to children has many other benefits. Wells (1986) found that exposing children to stories helps them make sense of their world by showing them the connections between events. Burke (1986) identified several areas in which literature can assist in children's intellectual development:

- Stories help children build bridges between the concrete and the abstract.
- Books help meet children's needs for beauty and knowledge.
- Stories assist children in developing perception and discrimination.
- Children develop a sense of story through exposure to books, allowing them to retell stories in

their own words or to create entirely new stories.

Perhaps the most important benefit of early story reading is that it helps stimulate language development. As Hall (1981) states, "Exposure to models of original and creative expression by gifted authors is essential if real language awareness and power is to develop in the elementary years. In using literature with children, the intent is for them to hear and read the best that has been written and to express their own thoughts and ideas" (p. 84).

In sum, then, when children listen to stories and are exposed to a variety of print—either at home or during their early schooling—they usually have greater success in learning to read and write and in developing a wide range of thinking skills. For children who have not had rich literacy-related experiences at home, story reading in the early childhood classroom is essential. In this chapter, I examine the theoretical and practical bases for using the shared book experience, a procedure that uses children's literature as a foundation for teaching reading and writing.

What Is the Shared Book Experience?

The shared book experience was developed by teachers of young children in New Zealand and is described by Holdaway in *The Foundations of Literacy* (1979). The approach was inspired by the traditional bedtime story. According to Holdaway, these read-aloud sessions provide the ideal setting for positive, satisfying exchanges between individuals. He goes on to say that "from the child's point of view the situation is among the happiest and most secure in his experience" (p. 39). This cherished activity normally involves only two people, a parent and a child. By greatly enlarging the size of a storybook and placing the resulting "Big Book" on an easel for all to see, the New Zealand teachers found that they could recreate the comfortable atmosphere of bedtime story reading with an entire class.

The process is simple. Using an enlarged version of a children's book, the teacher models the reading process by pointing to each word as he or she reads it aloud. When children become familiar with the text, they are encouraged to join in by predicting upcoming words or phrases, guessing at what might happen next in the story, or reading together with their classmates as the teacher points out the words.

At first teachers had to create all of these enlarged books themselves, but now a number of publishing companies produce Big Books. (Some even produce stories on transparencies for use with an overhead projector.) Although the selection of these materials is now extensive, teachers and children continue to enjoy turning their favorite stories into Big Books, scrolls, and story trains. In addition, text from other sources (poems, songs, riddles, jingles, jump-rope rhymes, and language experience stories) can be enlarged to contribute to a collection of classroom reading materials.

There are, of course, many approaches for teaching young children to read and write. In 1971 Aukerman iden-tified 76 different programs and procedures, and more have been developed since then. But the shared book experience is particularly successful, in part because it provides a comfortable atmosphere in which children can develop from listeners into competent and enthusiastic readers. The focus of this approach on reading aloud from children's books as the basic tool of early reading instruction adds both to its appeal and its effectiveness. The stories become the foundation for a number of language-related activities that help children grow in all aspects of learning.

Emerging into Reading

Clay (1979) has identified four abilities that are important for young children to have before they can become successful readers:

- First, children must have both a receptive and an expressive facility with oral language. They must be able to follow verbal directions and must have some understanding of a story as it is read to them. (Anderson et al., 1985, add that children must have acquired a basic vocabulary and enough of an understanding of their environment to be able to discuss what they see and know.)

- Second, children's visual perception skills should be reasonably well developed. In order to read, children must be able to attend to and analyze a set of complex visual clues. They also need to understand that the print conveys the message.

5

- Third, children need to begin to understand the concept of words; they need to know that the names of things and the vocabulary they use in speaking can be represented by a series of graphic marks called letters, and that these letters are grouped in clusters on a page. The spoken word "dog," for example, conveys an abstract notion of a furry, four-legged creature. To comprehend that the written letters d-o-g consistently trigger in people's minds the word and idea of "dog" is a second-level abstraction. This concept is difficult for many children to grasp.

- Fourth, children must learn to control their hand and eye movements to conform to the orientation of text. They must know the order in which to read print on a page (in English, from left to right and top to bottom) and learn that a visual scan through text cannot happen in the same haphazard manner as a scan of an illustration. The motor control necessary to proceed through text is vital to the reading process.

While these abilities develop through maturity and experience, some children master them more easily than others. Children bring to school a wide range of experiences and background knowledge. A teacher may encounter children who have no acquaintance with books, who have very limited speaking vocabularies, or who have no apparent knowledge of letters or words. The shared book experience and the activities it prompts help these children develop their basic vocabularies and oral language skills. The approach shows children that a story is conveyed through text. When the teacher models reading using a Big Book and points out each word as it is read, children become accustomed to the conventions of print and the way it is oriented on a page.

Of course, many children enter school with a great deal of knowledge about letters and words (Bridge, 1979; Hall, 1986; Teale & Sulzby, 1989). These children know the names of letters and are able to recognize certain words—perhaps their own names, the names of family members, or other words commonly found in their environment. For these children, the shared book experience can foster the development of more mature reading habits. Instruction can focus on strategies for predicting and comprehending, and follow-up activities can be designed to encourage these developing readers to attend to textual units, improve their comprehension, and create stories of their own.

The quantity and diversity of children's literature now available make it possible to adapt this approach for children at all levels of learning. The repetitive patterns of predictable stories are ideally suited for use with language-delayed children (Bromley & Jalongo, 1984) and children with learning disabilities (McClure, 1985). Coombs (1987) compared children's responses to two different approaches to reading aloud: the traditional approach, emphasizing enjoyment of story; and the modeled approach, using enlarged texts and shared book experience procedures. She found that the majority of children were more attentive and enthusiastic about the Big Books and gave richer retellings of the stories and recalled story elements more readily when shared book experiences were used. It was, however, the average and below-average children who exhibited the most positive responses to the modeled approach. Indeed, Coombs recommends that at-risk readers receive "extended instruction with this approach...as they begin to develop concepts about the reading process and its purposes" (p. 426).

Part of the reason this approach works well with such a broad range of children is that it makes use of abilities that nearly all youngsters share. Most five- and six-year-olds are naturally equipped with excellent auditory memories. They are able to learn songs, rhymes, and commercial jingles after hearing them only two or three times. This same ability can help them "memorize" text during the shared book experience. Initially when a page of a Big Book is turned, children may look at the picture and parrot the phrases they have heard. But as children hear the words of the story, they also see the teacher model the act of reading by pointing to each word as it is read aloud. Gradually the children will learn to attend to the graphic symbols and will come to associate the words they hear with the symbols on the pages. McCracken and McCracken (1972) summarize the process this way: "First, a child learns to love books and stories; second, he [or she] learns that books are to be comprehended; third, he [or she] learns to recognize words" (p. 18). And at every

stage the teacher acknowledges and praises the children's "reading-like behavior," thereby creating a positive learning environment.

An important aspect of the shared book experience is its sequencing of instruction. Children first become familiar with an entire story; teachers then use this familiarity to help students attend gradually to smaller segments of text—sentences first, then phrases and words within sentences, and finally letters within words. Goodman (1986) reasons as follows:

> Language is actually learned from whole to part. We first use whole utterances in familiar situations. Then later we see and develop parts, and begin to experiment with their relationship to each other and to the meaning of the whole. The whole is always more than the sum of the parts and the value of any part can only be learned within the whole utterance in a real speech event (p. 19).

The Benefits of Predictable Books

Although any children's storybook can be used for the shared book experience, predictable stories are the most popular. In predictable literature the language is simple and repetitive, often following a set pattern. There is also a close relationship between text and illustrations. The concepts presented in the stories are within most children's grasp (Rhodes, 1981). All of this helps young children apply what they already know about language to assist them in understanding the printed language in these books. Bridge (1979) explains further why reading from predictable texts is so advantageous for the emergent reader:

> The major value of the patterned language materials during initial reading instruction is that they enable the beginning reader to process the printed page in the same way as the mature reader, employing predicting, sampling, confirming, and disconfirming strategies from the first. The child is able to make accurate predictions of meaning and efficient use of visual information, thus practicing his or her skills for becoming a proficient player of the "psycholinguistic guessing game" (Goodman, 1976) of reading even during the initial phases of reading instruction (p. 507).

Language patterns commonly found in predictable books include four categories: repetition; cumulative structures; sequential episodes; and rhythmic language and rhyme (Tompkins & Hoskisson, 1991). In the first category, sentences, phrases, or episodes are repeated throughout the story. For example, in John Tarlton's *The King's Cat*, the phrase "the cat did not come down" (or a slight variation of it) is repeated 11 times. A cumulative structure is a pattern in which phrases or sentences are repeated and expanded, as in the familiar nursery rhyme "The House That Jack Built." In the third category, the structure of the story is developed through sequential references using, for example, numbers or the hours of the day. Eric Carle uses this structure in *The Very Hungry Caterpillar*, which depicts a caterpillar eating its way through the days of the week (and the pages of the book). Rhythm and rhyme, used to such good effect by Dr. Seuss, are also common patterns in children's books. Of course, these four categories overlap, and many predictable books employ more than one of these patterns.

These familiar language patterns, along with the inherent interest of children's literature, make predictable books an ideal medium for instruction in reading. In addition, studies have shown that such books can be an effective alternative to basal readers in helping students master language skills (Bader, Veatch, & Eldredge, 1987). Bridge, Winograd, and Haley (1983) studied two groups of first graders. The children who used predictable books for their reading instruction learned more of both the selected target words and the nontarget words than did the children who used basal preprimers. In sum, the predictable texts used most frequently with the shared book experience are effective and appealing teaching tools that guide children to a natural acquisition of literacy.

The Components of Language

Reading is part of children's overall language development, not an isolated classroom subject (Anderson et al., 1985). In building a program of instruction in emergent literacy, all components of language—listening, speaking, reading, and writing—are important. The shared book approach can help develop ability in each of these areas.

Listening. Reading books aloud to children is an excellent way to help them hone their listening skills. Rereading has even greater benefits in this area; as Clark (1976) notes, "Repetition of the same story read to a child has many values, not least the sensitizing of the child to the features of book language, which is probably a far more valuable preparation for school than any attempts at teaching the child phonics or even a basic sight vocabulary" (p. 104). When they become familiar with a story and are able to predict words and phrases during readings, children have an opportunity to reinforce their abilities in auditory comprehension. And when children join in with a choral rendition of the story, they have to listen closely in order to keep their place.

Speaking. The shared book experience also involves considerable oral participation. Children respond to questions about the story, predict upcoming words and phrases, guess at what might happen next, retell or reenact the story in their own words, and participate in choral readings of the story. All of these related activities allow the children's speaking abilities to mature.

Reading. Of course, the shared book experience helps children develop their reading skills, as described previously: first, children become thoroughly familiar with the whole and then they are ready to attend to the parts. A number of activities can be developed to teach specific reading skills, such as using a cardboard "mask" with a Big Book to block out surrounding print and let children focus on a target word or letter (Holdaway, 1979). Such activities can assist children in making the transition from parroting text from memory to being able to figure out the graphic symbols.

Writing. Although the shared book experience does not directly foster the development of writing abilities, it provides a great deal of indirect support. Many teachers notice that children incorporate themes and expressions from the stories they hear read aloud into their own writing. Holdaway (1979) has found that "the vocabulary and structures of the books begin to appear more and more in the children's productions of written language" (p. 134). Furthermore, teachers can develop a variety of writing activities based on the predictable texts to help children with this area of language. Encouraging children's efforts in writing this way also supports their growth in reading. As children invent spelling to create their own stories, they are learning phonetic associations. This reinforces the idea of focusing on small portions of text to analyze specific sounds and words in a meaningful way. And in becoming authors themselves, children move from the role of bystanders to that of active participants in their own learning.

In the shared book experience, all aspects of language work together to enable the child to acquire and develop literacy. The flexibility of the activities that can be developed from initial read-aloud sessions allows teachers to guide children in practicing a wide range of skills. In fact, the approach is so flexible that it can be readily integrated into other subjects in the early childhood curriculum and become the framework for the development of theme units.

Reading Takes Practice

"Children learn to read only by reading," says Smith (1978, p. 186) in a disarmingly simple but profound statement. Numerous studies confirm that a child's reading performance is directly related to the amount of time the child spends reading (Allington, 1977; Berliner, 1981; Guthrie, Martuza, & Seifert, 1979; Rosenshine & Berliner, 1978; Trelease, 1989; Wyne & Stuck, 1979). In addition to encouraging children's participation in the initial read-aloud sessions, shared book experiences can provide many opportunities for the emergent reader to encounter literature and engage in reading in a variety of settings.

After sharing a Big Book with the class, a teacher can, for example, make a tape recording of the story so the children can listen to it many times over, perhaps following along with their own copies of the text. Children enjoy hearing their favorites over and over again. According to Holdaway (1984), "The read-it-again phenomenon which produces for every child a body of favorite books probably accounts for the success of our very early readers and writers more than any other factor" (p. 20). Once they are very familiar with the story, children find its printed version less daunting. Teachers can also set up reading partners or hold individual or small-group conferences to increase children's opportunities to practice their reading, at first with favorite stories and later with less familiar texts.

Teachers often ask children to dictate their own stories based on the predictable books they have heard or read. These language experience stories can be used to make new Big Books, thereby linking literature to the lives and thoughts of the children. The creation of Big Books can become a class project in which all the children participate. These books can replicate stories not available commercially in enlarged format, or they can feature adaptations of favorite stories (perhaps with different characters and settings) or reflect entirely new stories created by the children. These creations add variety to a classroom library and give children extra material to choose at reading time. More important, children have an enormous sense of accomplishment when they participate in creating their own reading materials.

Language Learning: A Social Activity

Harste, Woodward, and Burke (1984) reason that "language and learning are social events. When the encounter which the child has permits feedback, then learning can take place" (p. 46). Social interaction and feedback take a variety of forms in the shared book experience and the activities it prompts. At the outset, the teacher works with the whole class during numerous oral readings of a predictable story and in many of the exercises that follow. Later two or three children are often encouraged to work together on different kinds of collaborative activities. Children are also able to work alone according to their own needs and interests. The teacher provides the necessary feedback by meeting with each child to learn about his or her interests and accomplishments, respond to questions, and guide the child to appropriate instructional activities.

The shared book approach also opens up the possibility of social interaction with older children. Working with an upper-grade teacher, the early childhood teacher pairs older and younger children for a variety of language activities. Many educators have noted the benefits of such cross-age reading/tutoring programs (Bloom, 1984; Cohen & Kulik, 1981; Fogarty & Wang, 1982; Labbo & Teale, 1990). The tutored child receives immediate feedback from the older student in a relationship that may not be as threatening as working with an adult. Tutored students tend not only to do better academically but also to express more positive attitudes toward school and academic subjects. Cross-age reading arrangements also benefit the tutors. The older children gain enormous confidence when they work with emergent readers; at the same time, they receive extra practice in reading. Trelease (1989) reported on one school district in which remedial fifth grade students tutored first and second grade children. He found that the self-images of the older children were greatly enhanced by participating in a program in which younger students regarded them as able readers.

Mavrogenes and Galen (1979) say that successful cross-age tutoring programs usually involve 20- to 60-minute sessions several times a week, but even sessions as infrequent as once a month or so will still benefit both groups of children. During these sessions different kinds of activities can take place:

- the emergent reader can read to the older student;

- the older student can read to the younger child;

- the older student can write down a story the younger child tells;

- the two children can work together to complete activities based on the reading;

- the two can echo read, with the younger child repeating each word after the older reader; or

- the older student can help the younger child write and "publish" a book for the classroom library.

Depending on the nature of the task, the tutors may need some training and may want to prepare for the session, perhaps by rehearsing a story they will be reading aloud. Both the tutors and the tutees usually take these sessions very seriously, so few behavioral problems occur.

The Teacher's Role

Sound pedagogical practices with respect to language instruction must be guided by a knowledge of children and how they learn. Educators have come to realize that literacy instruction should not be based on adult perspectives and cannot be broken down into a series of steps; rather, it must be based on a sound understanding of learning from a child's point of view (Teale & Sulzby, 1989). If the conditions for learning are comparable, the acquisition of reading and writing abilities can be similar to the acquisition of speaking skills (Holdaway, 1979). When teachers respond positively to attempts children make when they try to read, they mirror the favorable atmosphere that parents create when their infant begins to speak (Smith, 1973).

Regardless of their ability or experience in handling text, emergent readers can all achieve some level of success when they are involved in shared book experiences. From their first attempts at reading, the young children are set on the road to becoming readers confident in themselves and their developing abilities (Holdaway, 1984). Children thoroughly enjoy the predictable stories and the meaningful, goal-directed activities related to them. In addition, the reading takes place in a warm, relaxed atmosphere in which a sense of community quickly develops. Because children are not required to reproduce a passage word for word when they first attempt to read by themselves, they never experience a sense of failure. Much of the initial reading and responding is performed in unison, and shy or hesitant children are able to join in when they are ready. In short, the shared book experience provides an atmosphere conducive to learning.

The teacher is crucial in establishing this comfortable learning environment. Through scaffolding procedures employed at various stages in the shared book experience, the teacher offers young readers as much support as they require. Initially the teacher reads the entire story, thereby providing a model of reading techniques that the children can imitate. During a second reading, the teacher hesitates at some of the more predictable words and encourages the children to chime in. Over the course of continued readings, the teacher gradually withdraws support and the children assume more and more responsibility for reading the story.

In essence, the teacher serves as a model and guide, assisting each child in his or her own reading efforts. The teacher's role is that of a "facilitator who provides children with the opportunity to take responsibility for their own learning in stimulating and enjoyable ways" (Doake, 1985, p. 96). Spencer (1986) concurs:

> The teacher's role in early lessons cannot be to teach rules, but only to offer invitations to join an author in a text and to help the beginner breathe life into the page. If the teacher knows that pictures and print are the source of meaningful messages, then the pupil will expect to be read to, and will, in turn, work meaningfully on the things the teacher asks (pp. 61-62).

By implementing the shared book experience with emergent readers, the teacher is well on the way to achieving many of the goals of early education. Mass (1982) reasons that these first years of schooling should enable children to expand their knowledge of books and stories, enhance their communication skills, and develop their abilities in reading and writing. Shared book experiences are designed to help children make connections between what they already know about language and the more mature forms of reading and writing.

An Effective Approach

The Early Childhood and Literacy Development Committee of the International Reading Association, in conjunction with a group of associations involved in the education of young children, prepared a statement of concerns and recommendations about early childhood reading methods (reproduced in Strickland & Morrow, 1989, pp. 160-161). Among the recommendations are these:

- The language that children bring to school should be respected and used as a base for language and literacy activities.
- Literacy instruction should build on what children already know about oral and written language. Instructional experiences should be focused on the comprehension of meaningful text rather than on isolated skill development.
- Emergent readers and writers should be encouraged to take risks as they attempt to comprehend and use print. "Errors" should be regarded as a natural part of the development of literacy abilities.
- Feelings of success should be ensured for all children. These feelings enable children to regard themselves as people capable of exploring and enjoying oral language and print.
- Teachers should model reading and writing frequently for the children.
- Teachers should read aloud regularly from a wide variety of literary works, particularly from predictable texts that are familiar to the children.
- Children should have many opportunities to read and write independently.

- Reading should be integrated with the other components of communication (listening, speaking, and writing) and incorporated across the curriculum.

Martinez and Teale (1988) recommend further that the goal of an emergent reading program should be "to foster voluntary reading among the children so that they will develop positive attitudes and the inclination to select books for independent use and to sustain their attention to these books" (p. 568).

The shared book experience and its related activities fulfill these recommendations and, as a result, give young children a positive start in their acquisition of literacy. With this approach children extend their knowledge about print and strategies for reading and writing by observing teachers modeling these activities, by attempting to read themselves, and by interacting with others who are learning about language. According to Holdaway (1979), the shared book experience is designed to "support and not supplant the learning system of each learner, and will express itself in the respect and trust for the divergent ways in which children teach themselves the task they wish to master" (p. 202).

The flexibility of the approach is another of its great assets. The shared book experience can be used on its own as the basis of a complete approach for the teaching of reading, or it can supplement a basal reading program to provide children with essential opportunities to encounter real literature and to engage in experiences that will reinforce and extend what they already know about language. The literature used can be selected to appeal to the interests and backgrounds of particular groups of students, and follow-up activities to the read-aloud sessions can be designed to respond to the needs of each child. In other words, the shared book experience is comprehensive, flexible, imaginative, and stimulating, and provides teachers with an ideal basis for guiding children in their acquisition and development of literacy.

CHAPTER TWO

Getting Started

Reading aloud to children has long been a favorite activity of parents, grandparents, and other adults. Is there anything better than a bedtime story to bring a smile to a child's face, to stimulate a child's imagination, and to fill a child with wonder and joy? Reading aloud is also an excellent beginning to literacy instruction in the early childhood classroom. It is a relaxed, fun, and nonthreatening way to set children on the road to independent reading and writing.

Read-aloud sessions are the heart of the shared book experience. By using

Although the shared book experience offers an excellent approach to early literacy instruction, there are many other ways a teacher can facilitate learning. One of the easiest and most effective things to do is to create a classroom environment that is rich in print (Harste, Woodward, & Burke, 1984). McCracken and McCracken (1986) argue, "If we want to achieve universal literacy, our school goal should be to create an environment *cluttered* with print while demanding that children work with the written form. Insofar as the demand is real, the children will acquire literacy as easily as they acquire speech" (p. 6).

Features of the classroom—its walls, chairs, and chalkboards—can be identified with signs. Ask the children to decide on appropriate labels for these and other objects and for the different activity centers or areas in the room (Strickland & Morrow, 1988). The pictures that adorn the walls can be given titles or captions. Bulletin boards should be filled with children's artistic and written productions.

Not only are children's feelings of self-worth enhanced by displaying their work, but involving them in the creation of a literary environment will encourage them to view themselves as members of the literate community.

enlarged books, the classroom teacher can simulate the bedtime story experience and excite the children's visual senses with the story's illustrations. This chapter discusses Big Books and other materials required for getting started in the classroom, and describes procedures and activities designed to initiate the shared book experience. Although Big Books are the primary tool, most of the activities can be adapted for use with other forms of predictable literature.

The Basic Tools

The most important materials needed for the shared book experience are the books themselves. Although any book can be used, reading aloud to an entire class is easiest if the text is enlarged, as it is in a Big Book.

The number of Big Books required will depend on the teacher's overall approach. If the shared book experience is to be a major part of the emergent or developmental reading program, then having a number of enlarged books is best. Holdaway (1979), however, suggests that a teacher needs only a few enlarged books at the outset. Teachers will also need some kind of stand, such as an easel, to hold the Big Book so that all the children in the class can see it when it is being read.

Although other materials are useful when creating follow-up activities, a book and a stand are the only things needed to get started. But how to decide which books to use?

Easels make ideal stands for using Big Books with the entire class. Note that the pages will be easier to turn if the lip is removed from the easel tray. If an easel is not available, try using a chair. A chair makes a particularly effective stand for Big Books bound along the top since pages can be flipped over the chair back. Big Books can also be leaned along the chalkboard ledge, although this is a more awkward solution.

Selecting Big Books

One of the first things teachers need to remember in choosing books to share with a class is to select something they like themselves. Most teachers find that some children's books and authors appeal to them more than others; if they use these books, their enthusiasm will translate into effective lessons.

Another rule of thumb teachers should follow is to choose books that reflect the needs and interests of the students. An important factor here is the students' maturity; although a book appropriate for emergent readers in kindergarten may be at the right reading level for older at-risk students, its content probably won't be suitable.

Teachers should also be aware of the size of print in the Big Books. The words should be clearly visible from 15 to 20 feet (approximately 4.5 to 6 meters) away, depending on the size of the audience—that is, the number of children in the class or group. Furthermore, the children sitting at the back of the class will find it easier to see the words if they are at the top of each page, with the illustrations printed below.

Before spending a lot of money on an unfamiliar Big Book, teachers can familiarize themselves with the book's content by purchasing a regular-format copy or borrowing a copy from a library. In addition, copies of the enlarged versions are sometimes available in bookstores and at publishers' displays during teachers' conventions. They are also described in publishers' catalogs.

Many of the predictable stories described later in this book are available in Big Book format, and the annotated bibliography at the end of this volume provides descriptions of many more stories appropriate for young readers. Although this listing is far from exhaustive, it should give teachers some idea of the suitability and appeal of particular books for their students.

Making Big Books

When Holdaway's *The Foundations of Literacy* was published in 1979, the only Big Books available were those made by teachers who simply enlarged the texts of favorite predictable books. The situation has, of course, changed since then. But even though using commercially published Big Books in the classroom saves considerable time and effort, there are numerous reasons why teachers should still create at least some of their own materials.

First, not all the best predictable stories are available in Big Book format. By turning these stories into homemade Big Books, the teacher is better able to capitalize on the merits and excitement of exceptional literature.

Second, creating Big Books can provide many learning opportunities in the classroom. For example, when teachers are printing the text of predictable books onto enlarged pages for a Big Book, they can save some of the pages to complete in front of the children. The children will then have an opportunity to observe the creation of meaningful print. They will see that the teacher prints from left to right and from top to bottom; they will observe the spaces left between words and they will notice other features such as capitalization and punctuation.

Third, when the teacher shares the creation of a Big Book this way, the children will recognize the amount of work involved. Children who perceive that their teacher is doing extra work may be inclined to expend more effort themselves. This extra effort might be noticed in the artwork a child creates based on the book or in his or her attempts to read the text.

The greatest benefits of making Big Books, however, come when the children participate in the process. When children help create Big Books (or, indeed, any literacy materials) that are used and valued by all in the class, they are naturally very proud. They rightly feel that they are important, contributing members of the class, and this attitude positively affects their behavior and their learning. In addition, the material they help create—whether it is an enlarged version of a published text, an adaptation of a favorite story, or an entirely original work—is familiar and nonthreatening. The children are able to understand the text because they have made it their own. Moreover, when children create a Big Book, they engage in all the components of language—listening, speaking, reading, and writing. In particular, the connection between reading and writing is made very clear.

Finally, teachers often find that when they put forth the work required to create homemade Big Books, with or without the help of the children, they are inclined to use them more energetically and more thoroughly than they would commercial materials. Teachers' enthusiasm and pride in these books will be sensed by the children who, in turn, will be encouraged to do their best with these unique, tailor-made reading materials.

Teachers do not have to spend enormous amounts of time or money to create charming and useful reading materials. In fact, Big Books (and other materials for language learning) can be made using products that are readily available in most elementary schools. Holdaway (1979) suggests that just three Big Books are necessary at the outset. Only one of these needs to be a finished product, complete with illustrations; the other two might have the text printed on unbound pages, enabling the children to participate in the creation process by adding the illustrations.

Paper. Any large pieces of paper or cardboard can be used for the Big Book's pages. Holdaway (1982) recommends heavy brown paper (about 24" x 30", or 60 cm x 75 cm, in size); Heald-Taylor (1987b) suggests light cardboard or heavy cartridge paper (12" x 18", or 30 cm x 45 cm). Some teachers have found that chart paper works especially well because when the paper is turned over, the surface is blank but the lines on the reverse show through just enough to guide printing. Different types and sizes of paper can also be used and mounted on contrasting backgrounds.

The covers should be made from more durable stock. The back cover needs to be firm enough to keep the Big Book from folding over and falling off the stand or easel. It is also useful if the paper is heavy enough to support small pockets containing materials for activities related to the story. Both corrugated cardboard and poster board work well for the back covers.

A personal computer and a word-processing program can help you put together a Big Book in well under an hour. First, select an appropriate predictable story to read to the class. If it's close to Halloween, for instance, you might choose Bill Martin Jr's *A Spooky Story*. Read the original story to the children, and then ask them to help you compose an opening phrase for their own book, based on the story they've just heard. If you used *A Spooky Story*, the phrase you'd choose for your own book might be "From dreadful dark corners, from creepy crawly places, comes a...." Enter these words into the word-processing program.

A Big Book
in Short Order

Teaching Idea

Next, give each child a piece of black or dark construction paper. The children can use colored chalk or light colors of crayons to create spooky drawings. While the class is occupied with the artwork, call each child over to the computer individually to describe the scary creatures he or she is drawing. Type the child's words after the repeated opening phrase: "From dreadful dark corners, from creepy crawly places, comes a *big, horrible monster with green eyes and yellow claws and sharp, pointy teeth*."

Once you've completed the opening phrase with each child's description, print out all the text in large type and cut apart the entries. Then have the children paste their lines of text onto their own pictures. Each child can show his or her illustration and read the text to the rest of the class. When you're done, you can bind the illustrated pages into a book for the class library.

Printing the text. Words are normally printed with a broad felt pen. Teachers sometimes try out letters of different sizes and view word selections from various distances to judge the appearance and legibility of their printing. The text should be as close to the top of the page as possible so that children in the back of the group will have a clear view. Any text is easier to read when adequate space is left between the words.

Teachers should not rely on very young children to print the letters, although older children may be able to help with careful guidance.

The text can either be written directly onto the paper that will be used for the Big Book pages or printed onto smaller strips and then pasted into place. The text can also be entered onto a computer using a word-processing program capable of printing enlarged text. The

Figure 1
A Big Book Key-Word Page and Inside Back Cover

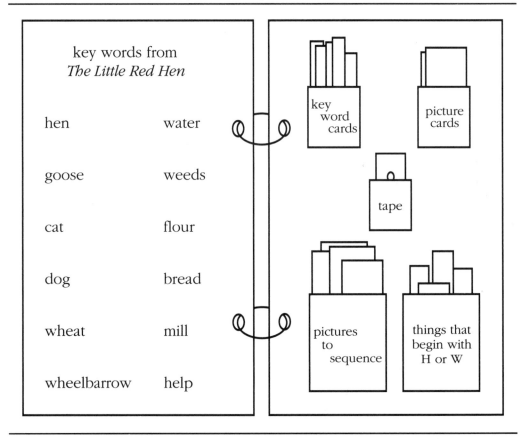

text should be printed using a plain font, one in which lowercase letters such as "a" and "g" conform to the familiar primary school "block print" style (that is, ɑ and ɡ).

Key-word page. Regardless of whether the text of a homemade Big Book is taken or adapted from a published predictable story or is an original creation, the teacher alone or in cooperation with the children should select some key words for special focus. The key words can be printed on a page at

the back of the book, facing the back cover (particularly if this is to be used for holding materials for related learning activities). Figure 1 shows a key-word page and the inside back cover for a Big Book based on Lucinda McQueen's *The Little Red Hen.*

Illustrations. For teachers who are artistically inclined, the creation of Big Books can be an enjoyable and rewarding exercise. Less talented teachers, however, need not feel embarrassed if their illustrations are not worthy of framing. Young children can be most understanding and very appreciative!

Teachers can use projection equipment to assist them with illustrations. An opaque projector will enlarge a page from a picture book and project it directly onto the paper for the Big Book. By moving the projector back and forth, the user can adjust the size of the picture to exact specifications and then trace an outline of the illustration's key features. Overhead projectors can also be used, but first the teacher must trace an outline of the illustration onto a transparency. The transparency can then be used to project the outline onto the Big Book paper.

Most children enjoy participating in the creation of Big Books by making the illustrations. A child can either draw directly on the Big Book page where the teacher has printed the text or work on a separate, smaller piece of paper. (The smaller size is more appropriate when the children's desks are small or when table space is limited.) When all the children have completed their drawings, the class gathers together and puts the pages into the correct sequence or glues the separate illustrations onto the correct pages.

If there are more children in the class than there are pages of text, teachers can still involve everyone in any of the following ways:

- One group in the class can make a Big Book to present to the rest of the children while other groups are creating different sorts of reading materials. The groups can rotate so everyone will have a chance at each activity.

- Some of the children can be asked to illustrate extra pages, such as the front and back covers, title page, dedication, preface (perhaps describing why the children selected this book to enlarge), key-word page, or the inside of the covers. Children can also provide additional illustrations to be sprinkled throughout the book.

- The children can work in pairs to create an illustration for one page.

Laminating. Pieces of text or illustrations that have been pasted onto the large sheets of a Big Book can be held firmly in place by laminating the pages. Laminating the covers and pages also helps protect a Big Book and increase its durability. A heat press or iron can be used to affix special, thin laminating plastic to both sides of the page, although it is easier to use self-adhesive, clear shelf paper. Both shelf paper and laminating plastic are quite expensive, however, so many teachers laminate only those Big Books that are particularly successful, ones they wish to keep year after year.

Binding. The easiest way to attach all the pages is to use a heavy-duty stapler to place several staples along the left side of the book. Metal rings, available in hardware and stationery stores, also work well. The advantage of rings is that they allow the book to lie flat as the pages are turned, making it easier for children to use the book on the floor or a tabletop. Rings are also more appropriate for Big Books that are bound along the top rather than down the left margin. A spiral coil can be used

O ne good way to involve all the children in creating illustrations for a Big Book is to divide the artwork into categories. A Big Book based on Alvin Tresselt's *The Mitten* is the focus of the description that follows, but almost any predictable story can be used.

Many Hands

A Big Book version of *The Mitten* would probably be about 15 pages in length; most classes have more than 15 children. Try this solution: Ask the children to name all the characters in the story—young boy, fox, mouse, wolf, frog, wild boar, owl, bear, rabbit, and cricket. You can also list objects that appear in the story—the old mitten, the sled of firewood, trees in the forest, and the new mittens. Then decide how many of each character and object will be required for the different pages of the Big Book. For example, the frog should appear on nine pages of the story, so nine frogs will be needed. Ask for volunteers to create the needed characters and objects. You might also ask two or three children to work together to create *all* the required drawings of a particular character or object. The children draw their characters and objects on colored paper and cut them out, ready to be pasted on the pages of the Big Book.

Children who finish their illustrations early can help draw some background trees or snowflakes directly on the pages of the Big Book or can work on the front and back covers and title page. When all of the illustrations are finished and cut out, the children can be gathered together to read over the pages.

This activity provides an excellent opportunity for children to learn the importance of different parts of a text as they decide which characters and objects are required for each page.

Teaching Idea

if a page-binding machine is available. The spines of Big Books can also be sewn together with heavy thread or dental floss (Heald-Taylor, 1987a). Once the book is bound, it is ready to be reread and used in all sorts of follow-up activities.

Making Other Reading Materials

Big Books are the basic—but not the only—tools appropriate for use with the shared book experience. There are a number of other materials teachers and students can make easily and use effectively.

Story trains and accordion books. Completed Big Book pages do not always have to be bound to be used by the children in the class. The pages can be mounted in sequence on a bulletin board or wall. Teachers can position an illustration of a train engine at the left of the display and one of a caboose at the right. This helps children see the beginning of the story and read the pages in sequence. The "story train" is an attractive, functional display, and the pages can be bound later, if the teacher wishes to do so.

Big Books that fold out like an accordion are made by taping the right edge of one page to the left edge of the next, and so on until all the pages are attached (Heald-Taylor, 1987a). The paper used for the pages of these Big Books must be stiff enough to stand without much support. Accordion books are ideal for standing along window ledges or on long bookshelves.

Transparencies. Predictable literature can be written on acetate sheets to be used with overhead projectors. The teacher can print the text onto the transparencies with permanent felt markers and let children illustrate the sheets with water-based markers. This makes clean-up easier and means that the transparencies can be washed and new illustrations created by different groups of children.

The sheets of the story should be numbered and coded so they can be sorted easily if they become mixed up with other transparencies. Each story should then be stored in its own envelope or box and labeled for easy identification.

Children love to use these stories independently or in small groups. The overhead projector can be placed on the floor in a quiet spot in the classroom, close to a blank wall. The children can project the acetate sheets for the story onto a piece of white construction paper or directly onto the wall.

Displaying and Storing Big Books

Just as toddlers ask their parents to read the same bedtime story over and over, emergent and developing readers will often return to a given selection of predictable literature many times in order to become comfortable and familiar with its text. Teachers who follow the shared book experience emphasize repeated readings of text and make books and learning materials available to children even after the class has moved on to something new. It is important, therefore, that children have access to all the different Big Books they have used over the course of several months.

Big Books can be placed over a metal or wooden rack normally used for drying clothes. One rack will hold many different books, all easily accessible to students. Several books can also be attractively stored in a graduated display rack made from corrugated board or plywood; this type of rack resembles a stepstool with very narrow steps and slots to hold the books in place. Tall shelves can also be used to store Big Books. Remember, though, that most Big Books do not have titles on their spines, so if they are stored on shelves, they will need to be labeled. Teachers can attach a title tag to each Big Book with a small length of string fed through a binding ring or staple. The tag will then dangle down the outside of the book and allow for easy reading.

23

- An early childhood classroom should contain many different kinds of children's books, not only the various forms of predictable stories and Big Books that are the focus of this volume. A large selection of paperback books is available fairly cheaply. Garage sales and book fairs offer used books at greatly reduced prices, and tattered covers can be replaced with the children's own creations. Old basal readers and children's magazines can be torn apart and recycled into a series of minibooks of collected stories. To augment a classroom collection, teachers can borrow books from the school library and rotate these on a regular basis to bring in fresh selections. Many local libraries permit teachers to sign out as many as 25 or 30 books at a time.

A teacher can designate an area as the classroom library. The basic requirement for this library is a set of shelves low enough for children to reach easily. Teachers often add other furnishings, such as an area rug, pillows, a display rack for special books, a mattress, or sofa. This minilibrary can easily become the focal point of an early childhood classroom, an interesting, inviting center that encourages children to explore and enjoy literature.

Story scrolls. Stories, poems, and song lyrics can be printed on sheets of chart paper and taped together to form long scrolls. Teachers can use two or more colors of marker to print the text in order to help children keep their eyes focused on the correct line. These scrolls are ideal for choral reading, although they are not suitable for children to use independently. Storage is easy: simply roll the scroll up, secure it with a rubber band, and write the title along the edge for easy identification.

Flip stories. A flip story can be created for any cumulative story or poem. The advantage of this technique is that it helps children focus on the repetitive nature of predictable text.

To create a flip story teachers need a piece of chart paper (or something similar) for each new line in the cumulative text. A flip story works from back to front; the last page is the first page that is read. Each succeeding page is cut shorter than the page before, so that the text from the preceding page is visible and the audience reads some of the pages again and again. Teachers often use chart paper for flip stories; it is thin enough to allow them to see the text of the page underneath and to place the lettering as required before cutting the pages to the appropriate length. Space for illustrations can be left at the top portion of each page.

Figure 2 shows the beginning of a flip story version of "The House That Jack Built."

Minibooks. A number of different procedures have been developed to bind and cover the books that children write themselves (see, for example, Graves, 1983, p. 59; Salinger, 1988, p. 172). One of the easiest for young children to use involves the advance preparation of a series of covers of different sizes ready for the children's stories.

First, the edges of a file folder should be trimmed so that the folder measures about 6" by 9" (15 cm x 22.5 cm) when folded. The outside of the folder can be covered with pieces of wallpaper from sample books, giftwrap, or contact

Figure 2
A Flip Story

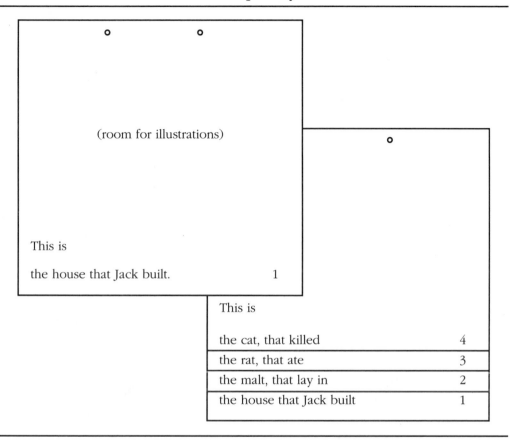

paper. The decorative paper should be cut larger than the file folder (about 14" x 11", or 35 cm x 27.5 cm, each) and folded over to the inside of the file folder. A piece of construction paper (8½" x 11", or 22 cm x 28 cm) is then glued to the inside of the file folder to cover the edges of the decorative paper. Children can write their stories on sheets of 8½" by 11" paper that have been folded in half, and these sheets can then be sewn into the prepared covers along the middle fold. The children's finished creations are then ready to be shared and added to the classroom library.

Pocket chart stories. Predictable texts are ideally suited for pocket chart stories (McCracken & McCracken, 1986), but because space in a pocket chart is limited, it is better to select stories with few words. The steps for creating and using a pocket chart story are as follows:

1. Each word of the poem or story is written on a strip of paper and placed on a chart fixed with rigid pockets. The teacher reads the story first from the book version and then from the chart, pointing to each word and encouraging the children to join in.

2. A duplicate set of word cards is prepared in a different color and children create visual matches by placing like cards on top of the originals. This can be done as a group exercise by distributing the second set of cards to different children. As each word is reread, the child holding the duplicate card places it on top of the original card. This continues until all the duplicate cards are in place.

3. The teacher creates separate illustration cards depicting selected words. These picture cards are distributed to different children who place the picture cards on top of the appropriate word cards, in effect creating a sort of rebus story.

4. Next the teacher removes the cards from the pocket chart and has the children try to match the picture and word cards without the aid of the chart sequence. Because of the practice they've had in the first three steps, children will usually be successful in reading these words out of context.

5. The last step in the pocket chart sequence is the recreation of the whole story. The empty pocket chart is brought out where all can see, and one set of word cards is distributed around the class. The children are then asked to do their best to rebuild the story, one word at a time. They all participate by chanting the story over and helping each other get the cards in the correct order. Then everyone rereads the completed pocket chart story as the teacher or a child points to the words.

To store several pocket chart stories ready for children to select and use on their own, a teacher can attach a shoe holder—the plastic or fabric kind with pockets—to the back of the pocket chart. Each pocket in the shoe holder contains the word card sets for a different story. To avoid the potential problem of the cards getting mixed up, the teacher can select a coding symbol for each story. Children love to help with this chore.

Procedures and Activities

Once the basic tools for implementing the shared book experience have been gathered together, it's time to begin using them with the children. Holdaway (1979) suggests these steps for introducing Big Books to the class:

1. Read a story to the children in order to catch their attention. On days when children seem restless, a familiar song or nursery rhyme is often effective in capturing their interest.

2. Display a Big Book. Using a pointer to follow the words, read the story aloud. Encourage participation from the children. In all like-

lihood, they will spontaneously join in, particularly at the most predictable parts.

3. Reread the story, but this time designate certain children to dramatize the actions, thereby increasing their involvement in the lesson. Keep the drama simple and use only essential props.

4. Conclude the first lesson by reading a different story or poem. Encourage the children to anticipate what will come next and to chime in as you read.

Holdaway also recommends holding initial sessions to about 30 minutes because of the limits of young children's patience and attention spans. Even the best lesson can lose its effectiveness if it goes on for too long.

These basic introductory steps can be modified in a number of ways to suit a particular class's or teacher's needs or to begin teaching certain skills. Teachers should try using a variety of activities. These activities should be fun; when children enjoy a reading experience, their interest in print develops and their learning will be positively affected. Teachers should remember to encourage children to become involved in the reading right from the start. This participation will often happen spontaneously, particularly if the reader has chosen a book in which the same phrase is repeated again and again. (Books such as Rose Bonne and Abner Garboff's *I Know an Old Lady*, Mirra Ginsburg's *The Chick and the Duckling*, Robert Kalan's *Jump, Frog, Jump!*, Ezra Jack Keats's *Over in the Meadow*, Bill Martin Jr's *Brown Bear, Brown Bear, What Do You See?*, and Lucinda McQueen's *The Little Red Hen* all have highly predictable texts that children will pick up quickly.) When children join in to predict words in a text in this way, they are developing semantic and syntactic knowledge and grapheme/phoneme awareness (Tompkins & Webeler, 1983); by encouraging children to make predictions, teachers are enabling them to become better and more independent readers. Spontaneous participation is also an indication of children's enthusiasm for the story—enthusiasm that will transfer readily into their desire to learn to read for themselves.

Descriptions of activities appropriate for the "getting started" stage follow.

Prereading Discussions

Discussing the content of a book before it is introduced will help children become involved in and learn from the text when it is presented. Teachers often bring in artifacts and pictures that relate to a predictable story they are planning to read aloud. Say, for example, the teacher is going to read Lucinda McQueen's *The Little Red Hen*—a story that mentions planting and growing wheat, making flour, and baking bread—to a class of emergent readers. The teacher might then bring to class wheat seeds (available at farm centers and through seed catalogs), wheat stalks (available at florists or craft shops), flour, and a loaf of bread. The objects are shown to the children to initiate discussion, which provides information that will help the children understand the story. The display and discussion of the objects can also help motivate children and focus their attention on the story to come.

Another advantage to this technique is that by setting up an exhibit of objects relating to a particular story, the teacher enhances the classroom's literary environment. A bulletin board or an extra desk can be used to display the objects, all of which can have identifying signs or labels. Pictures and children's drawings, accompanied by captions or short descriptions, add to the display.

Prereading discussions are also helpful for developing background knowledge, particularly in classes where the children have a wide variety of life experiences. After all, if children know little or nothing about a topic, it will be difficult or perhaps impossible for them to comprehend the story. To compensate for the diversity of children's backgrounds, teachers might extend the prereading activity just described by writing down some of the children's comments about the objects or pictures that have been brought to class. Teachers can also ask children to express their thoughts about a particular topic or character from the story. For example, before reading *The Little Red Hen* the teacher might ask the children what they know about hens. The children's remarks are printed on sheets of chart paper and mounted on the bulletin board. They will make attractive, meaningful additions to the classroom environment.

Developing Vocabulary

Before reading a story to the children, the teacher may wish to introduce words that appear in the text, especially key

Writing Down a Child's Words

- When a teacher writes down words that a child has spoken, the child is able to remember them and therefore read them, in part by recalling what he or she has just said. This helps a child move from listening and speaking to reading and writing in a natural way.

This procedure, called the "language experience approach," has been used successfully at the emergent reading level for many years. Language experience integrates reading, writing, listening, and speaking. According to Hall (1986), "The abundance of meaningful written materials in this approach can be a source of information for developing written language awareness, and children can also observe the conventions of written language such as word boundaries, left-to-right sequences, punctuation, and capitalization" (p. 39).

The teacher may use the chalkboard, chart paper, or a transparency to write down children's words. (When the latter two are used, the language experience story can provide materials and ideas for follow-up lessons.) Printing should be large and well spaced. All the children in the group should be able to see the words clearly.

As the teacher "takes dictation" from the child, he or she reads each word aloud. At the conclusion of the sentence, the teacher invites the child to reread the words. Some assistance may have to be given until the child develops confidence in his or her memory and becomes familiar with the procedure.

Because it takes a long time to record the children's words neatly, it is best to divide the class into small groups so all will have an opportunity to contribute. Each group can then share its story with the rest of the class.

words that may not be in the children's listening vocabularies. Even simple stories can contain words that are unfamiliar to some children. Many predictable stories also contain idiomatic or prepositional phrases with which children may need practice. For example, Mirra Ginsburg's *Mushrooms in the Rain*, about all sorts of creatures that seek shelter under a tiny mushroom, contains a number of expressions that would make an ideal introductory lesson.

The teacher can write the word phrases on strips of paper. From *Mushrooms in the Rain* the teacher might include these phrases: "peeking out," "hid under," "crawled up," "drenched to the bone," "huddled closer," "moved over," and "flicked his tail." The teacher then asks a volunteer to demonstrate "peeking out" (for example) from behind something. A second volunteer is asked to demonstrate "hid under" (perhaps by crawling under a desk). The children can be asked how they would feel if they were "drenched to the bone." Two children can demonstrate "huddled closer," and so on.

If children become familiar with specific words and phrases before the teacher reads the story, their attention and enthusiasm will be heightened.

Predicting the Story

When we are about to embark on a new experience, we often try to predict what might take place. Prediction can help us meet a new experience with greater understanding, appreciation, and confidence, even if our predictions turn out to be not altogether accurate. The same thing happens when we ask children to anticipate the content of a story. They will be inclined to listen to the story more attentively when they have developed their own expectations first and will therefore gain more from the read-aloud session.

One procedure teachers often use to introduce the shared book experience is to display the front cover of a predictable book (almost any one is suitable), read the title aloud, and then ask the children what they see on the cover. In effect, teachers are asking the children to predict the content of the story by analyzing the title and the cover illustration. The teacher should jot down the children's predictions on a piece of chart paper or the chalkboard. As the teacher is printing the predictions, he or she reads over each idea. At this stage, the accuracy of a child's prediction or guess is not important. All suggestions should be received as valid; each one warrants a positive comment. Teachers can always offer a response such as "That's interesting!" or "I wouldn't have thought of that!" even to the most bizarre prediction.

After the teacher reads the Big Book to the children, the class returns to the list of predictions and rereads each item. The children may wish to comment on the guesses they made. A prediction that did not in any way match the actual content of the story may have merit for another project—perhaps as an excellent idea for a different, original story. Teachers should make sure to offer such suggestions and positive comments frequently.

One teacher tried this technique with a small group of at-risk readers to intro-

Onne fun and effective way of introducing new vocabulary is with picture cards. Prepare a set of cards with simple illustrations of different objects mentioned in the book you are planning to read. These cards should be made with durable paper—cardboard or poster board works well—and should be large enough for the children to see easily. (If you print the words for the objects on the backs of the cards, the children can use them in follow-up exercises.) Cards like the ones depicted here would be appropriate for Eric Carle's *The Very Hungry Caterpillar.*

Teaching Idea

Place the cards along the chalkboard ledge or fasten them to a bulletin board. Ask particular children to find the pictures of objects you name. When a child finds the right picture, he or she should get it and hold it in a position that allows the rest of the children to see it. Save the most difficult ones for last, so that a child might be able to pick out the correct card by the process of elimination.

To increase participation, ask children without cards to identify pictures the other children are holding, or mix up the cards and repeat the exercise.

A s a variation on the prediction approach, try having children analyze a book's interior illustrations alone to create a version of the story. Choose a book with clear illustrations and little or no text. Mirra Ginsburg's *The Chick and the Duckling*—about a newly hatched chick that follows a duckling everywhere but gets into trouble when the duck heads for the water—is an appropriate selection.

Begin by arranging the class in small groups to give each child more opportunity to express his or her thoughts. With this activity, you don't want to read the title. Instead, display the book and quickly move to the first page of the story. A dialogue like this is typical:

Teaching Idea

Teacher: Sam, what's happening on this page?

Sam: A duck is getting out of its shell.

Teacher: Right! And now what's happening, José?

José: A chicken is getting hatched, too.

Teacher: What is he saying to the duck? Sally?

Sally: "Hi! Who are you?"

Teacher: Good! Maria, what's happening here?

Maria: The duck is running in the flowers and the chicken is running after him....

This version of the story has its inaccuracies, of course, but the children have made some reasonable predictions.

This approach is effective with all ages, including children as young as three or four. In addition to encouraging children to become involved in the story, this activity reinforces the idea that stories have meaning that can be conveyed through spoken language. Teachers can tape children's predictions for them to hear again later when they review the book on their own.

duce Ann McGovern's *Stone Soup.* Although not available in Big Book format (as of this writing), this clever story about a beggar who tricks a woman into fixing him a hearty meal is very appealing both to developing readers and to older students who are experiencing difficulty.

The cover shows a woman cooking over a pot and serving a man some food. The group of at-risk readers offered these predictions about the story:

- "The woman is cooking up some poisoned stuff to turn the prince into a frog."

- "No, I think she is making something magic to make the man extra strong."

- "I think he's wounded and she is helping him out. Look, he has a bandage on his foot."

- "Maybe he came to rob her. The bandage is a just a trick to get her to let him in the house."

None of these suggestions comes terribly close to the plot of the story, but all are valid predictions based on the cover and title alone. The teacher used the written versions of these predictions to teach a minilesson about quotation marks and suggested that the children use their ideas for original stories.

With repeated opportunities, the children will learn to make more realistic attempts at analyzing covers and illustrations. Later, children can be asked to speculate about the story on the basis of the title alone. Older children especially enjoy trying this. Eric Carle's *The Grouchy Ladybug*, Benjamin Elkin's *Six Foolish Fishermen*, Arnold Lobel's *A Treeful of Pigs*, Mercer Mayer's *What Do You Do with a Kangaroo?*, and Brenda Smith's *Wake Up, Charlie Dragon!* all have unusual titles and can generate fun and creative predictions.

Asking Questions

Right from the outset, it is important for teachers to engage children in discussion of books and to explore ways in which stories relate to real life (Teale & Martinez, 1988). This will help children learn that reading is relevant to them, while also encouraging social interaction, an effective backdrop for learning language. Asking questions about a book will also help the teacher ascertain if the children have adequate listening skills and sufficient background knowledge to understand the story.

Questioning activities are usually most effective with small groups so that each child has ample opportunity to participate. First the teacher shares the book with the group. He or she may then choose to close the book before asking questions about the story. If a child is unable to answer a question, the book can be reopened to the relevant page. Often the visual stimulation of the illustration will provide enough context for the child to respond. Remember that teachers need to be willing to accept a wide range of responses—a child's perspective of a situation can be very different from an adult's.

Teachers can design questions for use with specific books in order to develop particular skills in children. After reading a story such as Ann McGovern's *Too Much Noise* with a small group, the teacher can begin by asking the children a few questions based directly on the story: What was the old man's name? Why did Peter stick his fingers in his ears? Who did Peter see to get help? What kinds of animals did Peter bring into his home? Were the animals happy? What happened when Peter asked all the animals to leave? Was the house really quiet then? This can be followed with a few indirectly related questions that explore the children's background knowledge: What

T his procedure, based on the literature webbing strategy lesson (Reutzel & Fawson, 1989), is another variation on prediction. This time, however, children will be analyzing illustrations and text and predicting the sequence in which these should be arranged in order to make a coherent story.

First, select a predictable story that has a logically sequenced plot, with an obvious beginning and ending. (Edith Newlin Chase and Barbara Reid's *The New Baby Calf*, Mem Fox's *Hattie and the Fox*, Leo Lionni's *Swimmy*, Freya Littledale's *The Magic Fish*, Lucinda McQueen's *The Little Red Hen*, and Alexei Tolstoy's *The Great Big Enormous Turnip* would all be suitable.) Next, enlarge some or all of the illustrations (depending on the length of the book) and print the associated text on each page. (If you choose not to enlarge all the pages, take care that those selected are sufficient to tell the basic story.) In effect you are creating the "cars" for a story train, so you'll need to make an engine and caboose, too.

Now mix up the enlarged sheets and mount them where the children, either as a whole class or in small groups, can see. Read the text from each enlargement aloud and ask the children questions such as these:

- What do you see up here?
- Do you think these pages are in the right order? How do you know?
- How do you think the author would have arranged these pages?
- What do you think should come first? Last?

When the children decide on the sheet that they think should lead off as the first car of the story train, place this sheet to the right of the engine at the upper left corner of the bulletin board or the left side of the chalkboard ledge.

Often it is easiest for children to identify the beginning (next to the engine) and the ending (before the caboose) and then attempt to sequence the pages in between. You will probably need to read the text of the enlargements several times with the children before they are able to decide what might logically come next. When the children are satisfied that their story train makes sense, read the original book with them. The class then returns to the story train to compare the two versions and make any necessary changes.

33

is a donkey? How is a cow different from a sheep? Which of these animals is the noisiest? Besides making a lot of noise, what other problems could animals cause in the house? Finally, children can be guided toward more analytic thinking by soliciting their opinions with questions like these: If Peter wanted to keep one animal in the house, which one do you think it would be? Which one would you keep? What do you like most about the story? Are you ever bothered by too much noise? What do you do about it?

When a child responds to a question, teachers are advised to encourage the flow of social interaction with additional remarks and related questions. Ways to promote conversation include the following: (1) expansion—responding to the content of the child's comments; (2) semantic extensions—providing additional information based on the child's comments; (3) clarifying questions—seeking additional information about the subject; and (4) answers—responding to questions the child has raised (Snow, 1983). A glimpse of a typical classroom scene in which *Too Much Noise* is being discussed provides an illustration:

- **Expansion**

  Teacher: Which of these animals do you think is the noisiest?

  Seiji: The donkey.

  Teacher: Seiji, you think the donkey is the noisiest animal?

  Seiji: Yes, one time I heard a donkey at the zoo.

- **Semantic extension**

  Teacher: Are you ever bothered by too much noise?

  Wanda: My baby brother cries all the time. He makes a lot of noise.

  Teacher: Is your brother teething? Perhaps his mouth hurts and that's why he's so noisy.

- **Clarifying question**

  Teacher: When all the animals were in Peter's house, was he happy?

  Charlie: No.

  Teacher: Charlie, why wasn't Peter happy?

  Charlie: Too much noise.

  Teacher: And where was all the noise coming from?

- **Answer**

  Teacher: What do you do if it's too noisy?

  Tony: I put my fingers in my ears. What do you do?

  Teacher: Well, if I'm driving my car and the traffic is very noisy, I can't put my fingers in my ears. I play music then on the car radio because it's a nicer sound than all the cars and trucks.

These processes of social interaction are referred to as semantic contingencies—the continuation of topics raised by the child—and are of great importance in helping children acquire oral language skills (Snow, 1983). When semantic contingencies are part of a child's introduction to a book, they help establish parallels between learning to speak and learning to read while guiding children to an understanding of a particular text.

Choral Reading

Many poems and songs lend themselves to choral reading. Because of their rhythm, structure, and humor, rhyming texts are often easier to learn than prose (McCracken & McCracken, 1986). With choral reading, children make gradual approximations of reading the text without risk of personal embarrassment (Holdaway, 1979).

When the poem or song is familiar, the children can participate in the first or second reading; with unfamiliar text, the teacher may have to read the selection to the children several times before they are ready to participate in a choral reading. Children's magazines often have short, appealing poems that are ideal for choral reading exercises. Published collections of poems, songs, and nursery rhymes abound. In addition, many popular songs make excellent texts for choral reading. (Words are often printed on the recordings' sleeves, liners, or in their accompanying booklets. These texts can be projected in enlarged form with an opaque projector or the lines can be rewritten on a transparency.) The teacher can even play the song as a motivation for the reading exercise. Emergent, developing, and at-risk readers alike respond well to these sorts of texts.

Any enlarged reproduction of a text can be used for a choral reading (a flip chart is particularly effective if a cumulative poem or song has been chosen).

Grouping

Many lessons are more effective when the teacher works with just a few children. This is especially true when children are responding to questions or are creating language experience stories. The traditional way of grouping children—according to ability—is probably not the best, particularly for very young children. Indeed, this practice has been soundly criticized, for several reasons. According to Barr (1975, 1982), children in the lower reading groups are taught fewer skills at a slower pace. Ability grouping also affects children's feelings of self-esteem and colors their opinions of their classmates (Hiebert, 1983). Children, even first graders, are soon aware of the hidden labels attached to their designated groups.

Instead of standard ability grouping, try some of these alternatives:

- **Personality**
  Group children who like each other and work well together.
- **Seating arrangements**
  Each table or row becomes a group.
- **Draw numbers**
  Decide how many groups are needed and write a number—1 through 4 or 1 through 5 (etc.), depending on the number of groups needed—on a scrap of paper for each child. Each child picks a scrap of paper from a hat and forms a group with the other children who have the same number.
- **Sex**
  When only two groups are needed, it is sometimes simplest to group by sex. But be careful about using this technique, particularly if the activity involves competition.
- **Children's choice**
  Ask children to find one or two others with whom they would like to work.

The teacher may want to ask the children to close their eyes during the initial reading to eliminate visual distractions and encourage them to rely on their auditory sense. Then the first page of the Big Book, flip chart, story scroll, or other form of text is displayed. Next the teacher rereads the poem or song, pointing to each word and encouraging the children to join in. Eventually the children as a group will read the poem together without the teacher's prodding. Excitement and dramatic expression should be encouraged!

All children, even the youngest, enjoy choral reading activities. Different group patterns can be used: for example, boys can read lines one and three, and girls, lines two and four; or each row of children can read a different stanza.

Learning about Authors and Illustrators

The shared book experience calls for the use of many different texts and therefore offers numerous opportunities for teaching about the concept of authorship and the many styles used by illustrators. For example, the teacher can select several different books written by the same author or illustrated by the same person. (For this activity it is not necessary to use only books in enlarged format.) The teacher reads one of the selections to the children, then displays two or three other books by the same author or illustrator. To reinforce the idea that one person named Pat Hutchins created *Rosie's Walk* and *Good-Night, Owl!*, for example, the teacher can display a copy of another book in a totally different style, say Eric Carle's *The Very Hungry Caterpillar.*

Carle's writing and illustrating style are very different from Hutchins's, and children will be eager to point out those differences. The teacher can also track down two or more versions of the same story. The children can, for instance, compare Tolstoy's *The Great Big Enormous Turnip* with Janina Domanska's version of the same tale, called simply *The Turnip.* In addition, nursery tales such as "Little Red Riding Hood," "The Three Billy Goats Gruff," and "Goldilocks and the Three Bears" can be found in numerous different versions.

Teachers should also share biographical information about authors and illustrators. Often some information appears on a book's cover or jacket (there may even be a photograph); reference books on children's literature often have details on the lives and techniques of authors and illustrators.

Teachers can also ask the children hypothetical questions about authors and illustrators (Calkins, 1986):

- What questions would you ask if the author were to walk into our classroom now?

- Why do you think the author decided to write about this topic?

- What is it about the illustrations that you like (or don't like)?

- Do you think the author described everything clearly?

- What else would you like to know about the topic of this book? What do you think the author left out?

Observations about the author and illustrator should be made often. Children will gradually come to recognize similarities and differences in artistic expression and writing style. On other occasions the teacher can call the children's attention to information on the title and copyright pages, such as the publishing company and date of publication.

Later on, children will enhance their awareness of authorship and the elements of books when they participate in the creation of class books and write their own stories (Calkins & Harwayne, 1987). Graves and Hansen (1983) reason, "Somehow, readers who are also writers develop a sense of authorship that helps them in either [reading or writing] composing process" (p. 182).

Getting a Good Start

Predictable books can be introduced to children in many different ways. Some teachers prefer to develop and follow a standard procedure for introducing books. Others vary their approach in an attempt to meet the needs and interests of their students, address the attributes of a particular book, or use their own strengths and creativity to best advantage.

The most important thing with these initial lessons is to get off to a positive start. The shared book experience can help set all children on the path to becoming independent readers and writers. With this approach, children at all stages in literacy development participate fully in their encounters with literature right from the beginning and quickly begin to perceive themselves as capable readers and writers.

CHAPTER THREE

Following Up

Reading aloud to children does not, on its own, guarantee that they will learn to read for themselves. The shared book experience, however, does offer numerous opportunities for follow-up activities that develop from and expand on read-aloud sessions.

This chapter describes a number of different activities that promote the acquisition and development of literacy, some of which are extensions of activities introduced in the preceding chapter. Many of these activities can be used with a wide variety of children's literature—

predictable stories as well as other favorites. It is not necessary to purchase special materials or make a Big Book to implement many of these suggestions; pieces of literature (including poems and song lyrics) in almost any format can be used. It's up to the teacher to select those activities that are most appropriate for the children and that are compatible with the reading materials available.

For convenience, the activities described here have been grouped in three main categories: focusing on the whole text; understanding sentences, phrases, and words; and learning about letters and sounds. Note, though, that these sections are not mutually exclusive. When a teacher presents a cloze exercise to direct students to focus on words and sentences, for example, the children will also acquire some knowledge about letters.

Focusing on the Whole Text

With some traditional programs, the teaching of reading begins by focusing on the smallest units of text—that is, individual letters—and moves on to phonetic association. Only after that are words presented, first in isolation and then in short phrases and sentences. In contrast, the shared book experience is a meaning-oriented approach. The child becomes familiar and comfortable with the entire story, and the story becomes the primary context for understanding print in all its forms. Goodman (1986) explains:

> Whole text, connected discourse in the context of some speech or literary event, is really the minimal functional unit, the barest whole that makes sense. When

teachers and pupils look at words, phrases, sentences, they do so always in the context of whole, real language texts that are part of real language experiences of children (pp. 27-28).

The following activities use entire texts to help children strengthen their comprehension of whole stories.

Encouraging Reading

Anderson et al. (1985) note that children of all ages need to spend considerable time reading to become good readers. They cite studies showing that independent reading correlates with improved reading achievement and recommend that children spend at least two hours a week reading independently by the time they are in third grade. Teachers should therefore encourage many interactions with books in addition to conducting frequent read-aloud sessions. Beginning at the earliest educational levels, teachers can arrange for times during the day when children can read books on their own, even if this "reading" amounts only to turning pages, looking at illustrations, and making up or remembering a story to go along with the pictures. To foster independent reading the teacher can pair children so that each has a "reading partner." Children will sustain their interest in books longer when they are able to read and share with another child in the class. The selection of which book to read should always be left up to the partners.

While the children are working with their reading partners, the teacher can hold short conferences (five minutes or so) with some of the pairs. During a conference both children are given an opportunity to read aloud and share with the teacher; the presence of the partner gives each child support and reassurance. The attention they receive sends a strong message to the children: reading is important and the teacher cares about their interest in and progress with books. In addition, this procedure allows children to practice their oral reading and gives the teacher an opportunity to make an informal assessment of each child's progress.

Warm, sincere praise should be given to all children—the ones who simply describe the illustrations in the book as well as the ones who actually read the words.

Another way to increase the time children spend reading is to engage the entire class in sustained silent reading. A time is set aside for *all* members of the class—including the teacher—to read quietly on their own. This procedure has been practiced by teachers at all levels for at least 20 years (McCracken &

Playing Games

Teaching Idea

Another way to encourage reading is to demonstrate how fun it can be by making a game out of it. Children of all ages enjoy board games, and these can readily be adapted to strengthen comprehension of different predictable stories and reinforce vocabulary.

The description that follows is based on John Tarlton's *Going to Grandma's*, a book that is particularly suitable for at-risk readers. It tells the story of a family preparing to go on a trip to Grandma's house and the many things that can go wrong on the way.

To prepare for this activity, make a game board in advance that plots the route to Grandma's house, complete with delays, hazards, and unexpected advances. (A sample appears on the next page.)

In class, read *Going to Grandma's* to a small group of children (two to eight is best). Then show them the game board and help them read all of the directions printed on it. This will enable them to play the game more independently.

The game is played in a familiar way. Each player selects a token (an assortment of buttons can be used) and places it at "My House," the start position. The first player then rolls a die and moves the token the number of spaces indicated. If the player lands on a circle, his or her token stays on that spot, and the next player rolls the die. When a player lands on a square, he or she must read and follow the directions. The winner is the player who arrives at Grandma's house first.

The Game Board

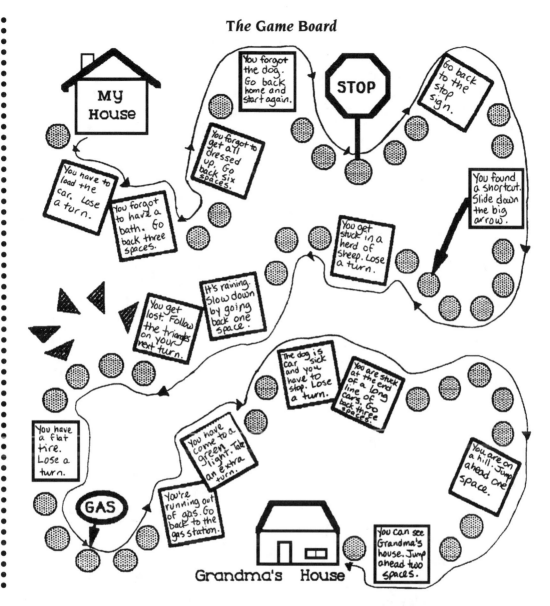

MY House

You forgot the dog. Go back home and start again.

STOP

Go back to the stop sign.

You forgot to get all dressed up. Go back six spaces.

You have to load the car. Lose a turn.

You forgot to have a bath. Go back three spaces.

You found a shortcut. Slide down the big arrow.

You get stuck in a herd of sheep. Lose a turn.

It's raining. Slow down by going back one space.

You get lost. Follow the triangles on your next turn.

The dog is car sick and you have to stop. Lose a turn.

You are stuck at the end of a long line of cars. Go back three spaces.

You have a flat tire. Lose a turn.

You have come to a green light. Take an extra turn.

You are on a hill. Jump ahead one space.

GAS

You're running out of gas. Go back to the gas station.

You can see Grandma's house. Jump ahead two spaces.

Grandma's House

McCracken, 1978). It works extremely well, but it does require the availability of a large selection of books and other reading materials.

Retelling the Story

In order to find out whether a child has understood a story's content, the teacher can ask the child to tell the story again in his or her own words. No special teaching strategy or workbook exercise has yet been devised that can match the effectiveness of this retell procedure.

Over the years teachers have found that feltboards can be useful in helping children retell a story. Characters can be cut from worn-out storybooks or be redrawn by the teacher and colored in by the children. Pieces of Velcro or felt attached to the backs of the cutouts will enable children to stick the characters onto the feltboard. These characters provide the children with a focus that helps them recall events and details of the story. Similarly, children's ability to recall a story's events will be enhanced when the teacher shows them the illustrated pages of the book. In all likelihood the pictures will help them flesh out their ideas and use words that are more "book like."

Teachers should offer support to children in their retellings. Verbal encouragement such as these prompts will assist children in expanding on their ideas:

- What is going on in this illustration?
- Why do you suppose....
- Right you are, but what happened just before that?
- And then what did they do?
- That's a good point. Tell me more about....

The teacher can repeat and expand on a timid child's quiet or hesitant words to show the child that his or her words are important and to offer support:

Joe: Went to sleep.
Teacher: That's right, Joe. He went to sleep. And then what did his wife have to do?

In the event that one child begins to monopolize the discussion, the teacher can stop the child with a friendly comment such as, "These are very good ideas, Paul. Now let's let someone else have a turn. Maria, what do you think happened next?"

Activities that ask children to retell the story should be repeated often, with literature of all kinds. With practice, the children will improve in their ability to recall events and details and will then be able to retell stories in a logical, sequential fashion.

Dramatizing the Story

When children dramatize a story, they are called upon not only to recreate the story's events but to pay attention to the correct sequence of those events. To do this accurately, they must internalize and fully comprehend the content of the story. Dramatization helps children refine and deepen their understanding of the story and, in the process, make the story their own. Research has demonstrated the positive effect dramatic play can have on children's early reading and writing development (see, for example, Christie, 1990).

Many predictable stories are appropriate for dramatic presentation, although those with repetitive dialogue are probably the best suited. (Susan Blair's *The Three Billy Goats Gruff*, E.B. Chance's *Just in Time for the King's Birthday*, Janina Domanska's *The Turnip*, P.D. Eastman's *Are You My Mother?*, Mirra Ginsburg's *Mushrooms in the Rain*, Pat Hutchins's *Rosie's Walk*, Veronica S. Hutchinson's *Henny Penny*, Anita Lobel's *The Pancake*, and Ann McGovern's *Too Much Noise* would all be good choices.) A typical procedure is for the teacher to read the story first and then ask for volunteers to act it out. The teacher then rereads the story, pausing for the volunteers to make the

Children's retelling of a story can take many forms. By varying the retelling activities used in class, you can keep students' interest level high.

Four suggested activities are described here. In each case, you should begin by reading the story to the children. You may find it more convenient to do the initial reading with all the children at the same time before dividing the class into smaller groups of five to eight members to implement the variations on retelling.

Retelling a Story
Four Different Ways

Teaching Idea

Oral Response

This description uses Arnold Lobel's *A Treeful of Pigs* to illustrate a simple oral response activity. The book tells of a lazy farmer who uses all kinds of tricks to get his wife to do the farmwork, but eventually she comes up with a trick of her own. This amusing story is popular with emergent, developing, and at-risk readers.

First, read the story to the children. Hold up *A Treeful of Pigs* and ask for volunteers to tell you the story. A response like this is typical:

Teacher: That's right, Peter, the title of this book is *A Treeful of Pigs*. It's by Arnold Lobel. Who can tell me what it's about? Juan?

Juan: Two people took a lot of pigs home.

Rainu: They were farmers—a farmer and his wife.

Peter: The farmer slept all the time and the wife had to do all the work.

Teacher: And then what happened, Rainu?

Rainu: He said he would get out of bed when the pigs climbed up in the trees.

Juan: She had to plant corn and she had to carry water and she had to dig holes.

Cathy: Then one day the pigs got lost and the farmer had to get out of bed to look for them....

An oral exchange like this is the basic form of a group retelling activity.

(*continued next page*)

Tape Recording

Make tape recordings of the children's retellings. A whole class divided into small groups will produce four to six different versions of the same story. As an independent activity, children can listen to recordings of their own and others' retellings. Copies of the book you're using should be available for the children's use when listening to the different tapes. Hearing different versions may help children discover ways to enhance their own retellings.

Sequencing Events

Putting events in a story into the proper sequence is difficult for many children. Young children will often recall the most memorable part of the story first, leaving out background information and events leading up to the climax. Sometimes children fail to see a logical sequence, as Juan did when he said "She had to plant corn and she had to carry water and she had to dig holes" in the exchange described previously.

To help children master sequencing, try writing their comments on strips of paper. This will allow their ideas to be easily reordered. During an activity like this the children will be recalling and helping to record events, reading what they have dictated, and reordering events into proper sequence to retell the story—all of which are major steps in the process of comprehension.

Create a Big Book

Help the children create their own Big Book version of the story. As they retell the story, help them edit their comments (if necessary) to make the version more readable. Write the children's words down as quickly as possible on any scrap paper and later reprint their comments on large sheets for a Big Book.

Select children to illustrate different pages, as well as the front and back covers and title page. There should be plenty of artwork for everyone to do. On the front cover and title page write the author's name, as well as "Retold and illustrated by the boys and girls in _____ class." Be sure to put the book in the classroom library.

appropriate actions and, with a little encouragement, supply the dialogue. A dress-up box full of hats, scarves, and other clothing for costumes will stimulate creativity in the children's dramatizations.

Many children enjoy this activity so much that they want to repeat it again and again. Experience suggests that two reenactments are a reasonable limit for one session. If children want additional opportunities, teachers can arrange a special drama time for the following day. Some children may also want to create dramatizations of the stories they have heard during their free-play periods. With encouragement, these children can put on their "play" about the story for the rest of the class. Small groups of children can be very responsible in planning performances, even when left completely on their own. Usually there is a quiet place in the classroom or hall where they can go off to organize and rehearse.

Adapting a Text

Having children participate in the creation of their own reading materials provides some extremely effective teaching opportunities. With the shared book experience this participation comes naturally. Typically, the teacher reads a predictable book or poem to the children. They respond favorably, and the teacher decides that the literature could become a much more useful classroom tool if it were in an enlarged format. Many predictable stories, including some of the best, are not available in Big Book format, however. It is therefore up to the teacher and children to prepare some of these reading materials for classroom use.

Some favorite children's books are too long to transfer directly into the Big Book format. Creative teachers get around this obstacle by reading the original story and then working with the children to create summaries of the main ideas to form the text for a Big Book. This teaches children the important skills of finding main ideas and summarizing, as well as giving teachers an indication of whether the children understood the essence of a story. Teachers might also wish to use this technique with stories from various anthologies, perhaps folktales that are representative of the backgrounds of the children in the class.

Asking children to adapt or extend a predictable story will also help them strengthen their comprehension of the original text. In addition, the new stories they create are ideal texts for classroom reading material. What feelings of pride the children will experience when they realize their accomplishments and put their own Big Books to good use!

Many predictable stories lend themselves quite easily to adaptations or extensions. A book like P.D. Eastman's long-time favorite *Are You My Mother?*, for example, can be used to create a new story about what happens to the baby bird on the day *after* he had his adventures in finding his mother. The teacher helps the children with their creation by posing guided questions (Cazden, 1988) that direct them to keep their responses within a story framework:

Teacher: Let's pretend it's the next day and the baby bird has just woken up. What does he say? Pedro?

In this activity, a favorite with children of all ages, a predictable story is adapted to create a "television" show. The first step is to make a TV. Find a box at least 14" x 16" x 8" (35 cm x 40 cm x 20 cm) and decorate it on the front with buttons and knobs to resemble a TV. Cut out four slots, two in the front and one on each side, as shown below. Each slot should be a little longer than the width of the paper you will be using (probably about 12", or 30 cm).

Shelf paper is ideal for this activity. With a pen or marker, divide the paper into frames as wide as the space between slots on the front of your TV box. One frame is required for each page in a book. Leave extra paper at both ends of the story to help keep the paper in the slots.

The first frame or two should announce the show, giving the story's title and the credits—the author's *and* children's names. Then print the text on each frame (it may need to be edited so that one page will fit on one frame). The letters should be large enough to be seen from 6 to 10 feet (2 to 3 meters) away. Ask the children to illustrate each frame.

Now feed the end of the paper roll into the slot on the left face of the box, out through the slot on the left of the TV's front, back in the right-hand slot, and finally out through the slot on the right face. The children who created the television version of the story read the frames as they roll by, while the rest of the class looks on and listens.

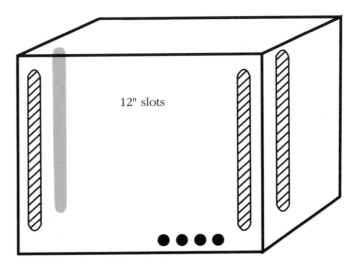

12" slots

Pedro:	"I'm hungry. I want my breakfast."
Teacher:	And then what does the mother do?
Aldona:	The mother bird goes to look for food.
Teacher:	But the mother is gone for a long time. What does the baby bird do?
Bonnie:	He waits and waits, and then he goes to look for her.
Teacher:	And who does he meet?
Tom:	He sees a cat. "Did you see my mother?"
Teacher:	Henri, what does the cat say?
Henri:	"No, I didn't see your mother. Ask somebody else."
Teacher:	And now who does he meet?

The purpose of the teacher's questions is to provide as much assistance as the children require to enable them to produce a repetitive and predictable story. (Note that if a child has had limited experiences in listening to stories or is a second-language learner, more support over a longer period will be required to ensure his or her success.)

It is easiest to use a tape recorder to capture the conversation. The children's comments (and any of the teacher's comments or additional words necessary to make a coherent story) are then transcribed, divided into page-length segments, and printed or glued onto large sheets of paper. (Printing words directly on Big Book pages would require the children to sit for too long.) Once the children illustrate the pages, the Big Book is bound and added to the classroom library.

The text can also be reproduced in a smaller size to make minibooks for everyone in the class. Each child can then follow along in his or her own minibook as the teacher reads the Big Book aloud. A choral reading or a time for children to work with their reading partners to illustrate and create covers for their minibooks could follow. If the text is tape recorded, children can also use their minibooks in independent activities at the listening center.

Language Experience Activities

When children's own words are written down by the teacher and used for various activities, literacy learning can be greatly enhanced. Teachers can guide these language experience opportunities to further children's comprehension of predictable stories. In addition, the children's words about these stories will give the teacher a good indication of how well the text has been understood.

One particularly effective way to enrich comprehension is to focus on themes. After reading a selection of predictable literature, the teacher can list a theme or idea from the story at the top of a piece of chart paper. The children are then invited to make comments about this theme. The teacher prints their words on the paper, reading each word aloud as he or she does so. When a fair number of comments have been offered and printed, the teacher and children read through the entire chart together.

The chart should then be posted in the room. As an independent activity, a child and his or her reading partner can read the chart again to see how many of the words they can recall by themselves. The teacher can also use the words on the chart to demonstrate ways of expanding words and phrases into full sentences. Say, for example, that the teacher has read Christina Rossetti's *What Is Pink?* and asked the children to comment on the related theme of "yellow things." The children are likely to respond in few words—"banana," "my beachball," "Mom's car," or "our kitchen table." The teacher should write these words down as they are spoken, but on the following day children can be asked to develop their words into complete sentences, ideas, and eventually stories.

The language experience approach can also be used in a more individualized way to foster the acquisition of literacy and develop comprehension of text. Having children create a picture based on an experience and write down their comments about their artwork has long been a favorite activity of early childhood teachers. It can also become an excellent follow-up activity to a read-aloud session if the teacher asks children to base their artwork on the predictable literature that has been shared. (Note that this seemingly simple activity requires a great deal of time and is best undertaken in small groups.)

Children are asked to respond to the story by drawing their favorite part. Then each child is encouraged to tell about his or her drawing. The teacher writes down the child's exact words, perhaps on a piece of paper designed to fit as a caption at the bottom of the child's drawing. As the teacher prints the child's words, he or she points to and reads each word again. Next the teacher invites the child to read the words back as he or she points to each word in turn. Children should then be given time to share their artwork and descriptive words with their classmates. Finally the pictures are posted for all to see (they make excellent bulletin board displays) or fastened together to create a special class book.

Teachers find that after this activity has been undertaken a couple of times, children will begin to write their own captions and descriptions for the pic-

Books and Themes

Here are some predictable books with themes that are suitable for language experience charts.

This Is the Place for Me (Joanna Cole): What would you like to have in a new home?

What Can You Do with a Shoe? (Beatrice de Regniers): What can you do with a shoelace [ball, cardboard box, etc.]?

Millions of Cats (Wanda Gag): One and many [singular and plural forms of familiar objects].

Boss for a Week (Libby Handy): What would you do if you were boss for a week?

Over in the Meadow (Ezra Jack Keats): Over in the schoolyard [park, shopping center, etc.].

Leo the Late Bloomer (Robert Kraus): What can you do well? Or, what would you like to be able to do?

There Was a Crooked Man (Mother Goose): Things that are crooked or bent.

What Is Pink? (Christina Rossetti): Things that are yellow [green, red, etc.].

tures they draw. This can happen spontaneously as children copy the actions they observe their teachers performing (Allen, 1976).

Understanding Sentences, Phrases, and Words

When a predictable book has been read repeatedly, many children will be able to read it back, often word for word. But this does not necessarily mean that the children know each word in isolation or could recognize any of them in a different context. The text could simply have been memorized (at this age most children have well-developed auditory memories) or the illustrations could be providing clues.

The activities described in this section take advantage of young children's many abilities and interests to help them focus on small units of text—sentences, phrases, and words. Many of these are independent activities that can be introduced to a small group and then placed in centers where a child can work alone (or with a partner).

Masking

Holdaway (1979) recommends that teachers create a cardboard mask that can be used to highlight phrases, words, or letters on the pages of Big Books. A mask, an example of which is illustrated in Figure 3 on the next page, can help children focus on one part of the text.

To make a mask like the one shown in Figure 3, first cut a long, rectangular window out of the center of two pieces of cardboard. The vertical measure of the window should be slightly greater than the height of the text in the average Big

Book. Staple the two cardboard pieces together on three sides. Next, cut a strip of cardboard a little wider than the window and slip it between the pieces of cardboard at the unstapled side. The window can be adjusted to reveal one letter, a word, or a short phrase by sliding the strip back and forth; the larger pieces of cardboard mask out the surrounding text. (If the text has been printed on a transparency for use with an overhead projector, sheets of paper can be placed to isolate segments of the text.)

When the children have become familiar with the story in a Big Book, the teacher selects one page and rereads it with the help of the class. Then the teacher uses a mask to isolate a key word or phrase on the page and asks for a volunteer to read it. Whenever a child has difficulty with a word or phrase in isolation, the teacher can remove the mask and reveal the whole text. In all likelihood the child will recognize the word or phrase in the context of the complete sentence and with the help of the illustration. If children continue to have difficulty recognizing words in isolation, teachers can turn to easier Big Books—those with relatively few words and simple language structures—before repeating the masking technique. They can also read the entire story over repeatedly, and perhaps tape-record it so the children can listen to the story any number of times on their own.

Cloze Activities

Cloze is a very versatile procedure in which students are asked to supply words deliberately omitted from a text. Taylor (1953) first used cloze as a tool to

Figure 3
Masking Peter Piper

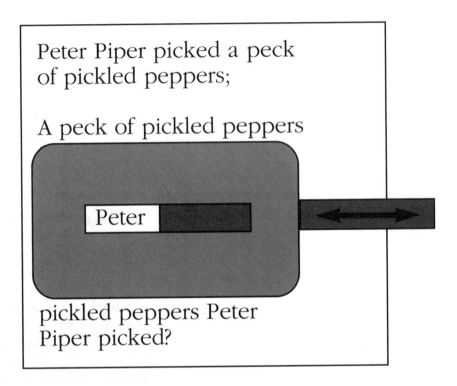

Peter Piper picked a peck of pickled peppers;

A peck of pickled peppers

Peter

pickled peppers Peter Piper picked?

determine the readability of a given text. Cloze exercises have also been used to determine students' reading levels, to help children increase their speaking vocabularies, and to guide children in understanding the structure of language. Holdaway (1979) recommends using a variety of cloze activities with the shared book experience. He reasons that "the easiest way of inducing meaningful language activity is to provide gaps in an otherwise complete flow of language" (p. 101).

The cloze procedure helps children with both word recognition and vocabulary. Perhaps more important, though, is the way cloze can demonstrate to children that the message comes from the print and not the illustration, that there is a one-to-one correspondence between the spoken and the written word, and that print is read in a particular direction.

Making and Using Tapes

Audiotapes of predictable stories have many uses in the early childhood classroom. Children can listen to them for pleasure, or more structured activities can be developed for their use. Listening centers where children can hear the tapes (and follow along in copies of the books, if they choose) should be established. Although all children can benefit from listening to the recordings, Holdaway (1979) suggests that children who are experiencing difficulty will profit most from repeated sessions.

Holdaway also suggests that because so many early childhood teachers are women, at least some of the tapes should be recorded by a man: "We use mainly male voices because many of the slower children are boys and they must not get the idea that reading is a feminine occupation" (p. 73). Regardless of the speaker's sex, however, the story should be recorded in a clear, expressive voice at a fairly slow pace. Children will follow the text word for word in their books, and obviously this is easier if the story is read slowly. The person creating the tape might also pause at the end of each page to allow time for the children to turn the pages of their books.

Some publishing companies produce Big Book packages containing one enlarged copy of the predictable book, several small copies, and a tape of the story.

Cloze activities fall into two broad categories: oral and visual. In an oral cloze activity a teacher might read a predictable text through and then, during a second or third rereading, pause at and point to selected key words. The children will usually be able to supply the missing word or phrase, especially if the teacher looks at them with an expression of expectation. Initially the teacher supplies all but one or two key words so the children can experience success right from the beginning. With each reading of the story, the teacher can pause more frequently and can expect the children to complete entire phrases. The children increasingly assume more active roles.

The most common way to implement a visual cloze activity is for the teacher to print a selection of sentences from a predictable book on the chalkboard. Each sentence is printed exactly as it appears in the book, but a word is left out and replaced by a blank line: "Mary had a little _____ whose fleece was white as snow." The children, with assistance from the teacher, read the sentence and try to supply the missing word.

Often it is more desirable to write cloze sentences on strips of paper rather than on the chalkboard. This allows teachers to repeat the exercise again on different days and lets children replicate the activity on their own. If all the children are to be included in this sort of cloze activity, the strips will have to be quite long (about 24", or 60 cm) to accommodate printing large enough to be seen clearly by children at the back of the room. Also necessary are cards or slips of paper, cut to fit into the blank lines on the cloze sentence strips and containing the missing words.

Say the teacher prepares these cloze sentence strips, based on Mem Fox's *Hattie and the Fox*:

- Hattie was a big black _____.
- And Hattie said, "Goodness _____ me!"
- But the _____ said, "Moo!"

51

Asa variation on the oral cloze activity, special audiotapes can be created for independent use by children in the listening center. This activity works best if simple, familiar texts—such as Mother Goose rhymes—are used.

Select several of the most popular rhymes to be read onto a tape. Record each rhyme intact for the first reading, and then read the same poem with a few key words omitted. This cloze version should have fairly long pauses where the words have been left out, to give the children enough time to say the missing words or phrases out loud. Make sure that copies of the rhymes' texts are available in the listening center so children can follow along with the taped reading. If more than one rhyme is read, remember to ensure that the texts are in the same order as they are read on the tape!

The teacher would then also need to prepare appropriate-sized cards with the words "gracious," "cow," and "hen" written on them.

The teacher displays the entire set of cards and then displays one cloze sentence strip. The children read all the words on this strip, with the teacher's help. If necessary, the original predictable book can be used as a reference. One child can then volunteer to pick out the card slip that best completes the sentence and secure it on the blank line with a paper clip. Another child can confirm the choice by checking in the book.

This activity is easily extended to provide more learning opportunities. After a word has been correctly identified, for example, children can be asked to think of other words that would make sense in the same sentence. Children might also be asked to choose an incorrect word to yield a humorous result: "But the ___hen___ said, 'Moo!'"

As a variation on this activity, teachers can draw simple illustrations on the backs of the cards, corresponding to the words on the front. (Obviously this will work only with certain words.) The cloze strip then becomes a rebus sentence. This will enable the children to use this activity independently because they can consult the illustrations for clues. If the rebus sentences are attractive enough to warrant display, they can be mounted on a bulletin board, low enough for the children to reach so the area can serve as an independent activity center.

Concentrating on Key Words

Teachers will occasionally want children to focus on particular words from a predictable story, song, or poem. These "key words" may be those that the teacher feels will be unfamiliar to most of the children, those that can be represented by pictures, those that demonstrate actions, and so on.

Bingo, a game popular with children of all ages, can be adapted to become a learning activity to reinforce sight recognition of key words. The example that follows is based on Robert Kraus's *Leo the Late Bloomer*, a good choice for at-risk readers, but almost any children's book could be used. If you are going to make more than one key-word bingo game, prepare the game boards and key-word cards in different colors for each book so they can be easily separated.

First choose 16 to 20 key words from the text and print them on small durable cards (index cards work well). Now make a game board for each child in the group from a piece of cardboard or poster board, approximately 9 inches (23 cm) square. Draw lines on each board to divide it into nine sections and print one key word in each section. The words on each board should be slightly different from the words on other boards, as shown in the example below. The children will also need squares of paper or disks to cover the words on the game boards. These pieces can be kept in envelopes clipped to each game board.

Key-Word Bingo

Teaching Idea

read	write	draw
word	bloomer	father
mother	signs	day

television	time	late
watched	spoke	draw
night	day	word

The teacher uses the key-word cards and calls out one word at a time. The players look for the word on their bingo boards; if it appears, they cover it with a disk or square of paper. The first child to cover all the words calls out "Bingo!" and the teacher checks to see if the game has been won. At the beginning many of the children will be unable to recognize a word when it is called. To alleviate this problem, first read the word aloud and then turn the card around so the children can see it. After you have played a few rounds, children can play the game by themselves with one of them designated as "teacher" to call out the key words.

Key words can be printed on the inside back cover of commercial Big Books or listed on a separate page at the end of a homemade version. They can be printed at the bottom of story scrolls in a contrasting color or boxed at the side of a transparency. When words are highlighted in this way teachers can refer to them often, if only to ask children simple questions about their meanings.

A number of follow-up activities that will help children focus on key words are also possible. In addition to listing the words, teachers can, for example, create a corresponding set of key-word cards. As these cards will be used by small groups and individuals, they do not have to be very large—3 inches by 8 inches (8 cm x 20 cm) should be large enough.

As an independent activity, a child can spread all the key-word cards out for easy visibility, then turn to the page in the Big Book where the key words are listed and place a word card next to the corresponding key word on the page. For a more challenging variation, the child can look through the book and create matches between the key-word cards and the words printed in the text. If the teacher creates two sets of key-word cards, children can play a version of "Concentration." The cards are spread out face down in a large square and each child tries to find a match by turning over two cards at a time. If no match is made, the cards are turned back over; if a match is made, the child removes the cards from the square. The game continues with the players taking turns until all matches are made and all the cards are removed.

The children do not have to be able to read the text or recognize key words in isolation to do any of these activities. And because the activities help children become more sensitive to text and word and letter order (and eventually add to their sight-word vocabularies), they are ideal for emergent readers.

A similar activity can be used with developing readers. First the teacher must create another set of cards with pictures to represent each of the key words. Then the child matches the key words to the corresponding pictures. If the child is able to create a match, he or she may well remember the word in other contexts.

Matching Illustrations and Text

Matching activities can be extended beyond a strict focus on key words. When children are able to match words, they are demonstrating abilities in visual recognition. When they match a picture of an object or scene to the appropriate word or caption, they are demonstrating that they are learning to read the word or words. Children benefit from repeated practice with this sort of activity.

Matching illustrations to text can be a follow-up activity to a read-aloud session of many predictable books. This activity can be used with all ages, depending on the complexity of the literature selection. Teachers will need to use durable paper (index cards, for example) to create two sets of cards. On one set of cards, the teacher draws pictures for each page or significant event in the story, or pastes on selected illustrations cut from worn copies of the book. The text is printed on the second set of cards or, if the text is too long, a summary or caption can be substituted. (Laminating the completed sets will increase their durability.) Children can then match the illustration cards to the corresponding word or phrase cards, using a copy of the book as a reference, if needed. To make this an independent, self-correcting activity, the left edge of the illustration cards can be cut to mesh with the right edge on the corresponding text cards, as for a jigsaw puzzle.

Predictable texts presented as pocket chart stories are useful for word-to-word matching activities. With pocket chart stories, children simply match a set of word cards to those displayed on the chart. As a variation, a corresponding set of cards with illustrations can be prepared, and children can match these to the appropriate words, placing them on the chart to create a rebus story.

The pocket chart story is also extremely useful for demonstrating different language lessons. Minilessons in different language skills are most appropriate when the teacher perceives a need among the children in the class. When the teacher meets with children for conferences, he or she often realizes that a specific lesson about a particular facet of language would be beneficial. Pocket charts are a means of providing visual back-up for these lessons.

Sentences that appear in the past tense on the pocket chart, for example, can be easily altered to the present tense with a few substitute word cards. This demonstration will reinforce a basic lesson in verb tense. The children can be shown how to turn a declarative sentence into a question if the teacher pre-

Storing Learning Materials

When a teacher has assembled a substantial collection of Big Books and other reading materials—each with its own activity cards, tapes, games, or related activities—storage can begin to be a problem. Many teachers devise a code to identify each Big Book and all accompanying learning activities. For example, a *Rosie's Walk* Big Book, as well as the different games, the tape recording, and the other learning materials made to go with it, could have two red circles affixed to each piece; another Big Book and its accompanying materials could be identified with blue squares. This sort of coding will help the teacher sort out the sets of materials when they become mixed through enthusiastic use. Coded identifications can also be made with colored markers or rubber stamps. Children love to assist the teacher with this sort of coding; with a few instructions, a small group of children can have an entire assortment of materials coded in very little time.

The inside back cover of a Big Book is an ideal place for holding a limited number of learning materials. Manila envelopes or rectangles cut from heavy board and stapled in place can be used to create pockets to hold key-word cards, tapes, and other small learning materials. Of course, this will work only if the back cover is firm enough to support the contents of the pockets.

Games and larger learning materials can be kept separate from Big Books in boxes or Manila envelopes. Pencil boxes make ideal containers for key-word cards or small games; boxes used for ditto stencils are perfect for some of the larger games. Box tops can be painted or decorated with wallpaper. Each storage envelope or box should be labeled with the name of the activity and coded with the symbol relating it to its Big Book. Teachers may also keep a Big Book and all its learning materials together in a large carton.

pares additional word cards (and, of course, cards with question marks). By asking children to substitute random words in the existing sentences on the pocket chart, the teacher will be assisting them in understanding parts of speech. They will come to realize that only certain word substitutions make sense: "Teddy bear, teddy bear, touch the ground" from a popular jump-rope rhyme could be altered to "touch your shoes" or "touch the light," but not "touch the say" or "shoes your ground."

Phrase Strip Dialogue

Many predictable stories repeat phrases of dialogue many times over. This can be put to great advantage over the course of rereadings of the story, to the considerable delight of the children. Children love this feature, since it lets them chime in during rereadings of the story. Teachers can take advantage of this natural tendency by creating phrase strips with pieces of dialogue from a story to help the children focus on print. This idea, a variation of the popular Readers Theatre technique, is appropriate for all levels, depending on the length of the dialogue phrases and their complexity. Eric Carle's *Have You Seen My Cat?*, E.B. Chance's *Just in Time for the King's Birthday*, Mem Fox's *Hattie and the Fox*, Mirra Ginsburg's *The Chick and the Duckling*, Pat Hutchins's *Good-Night, Owl!*, Anita Lobel's *The Pancake*, and Rosemary Wells's *Noisy Nora* are examples of books with repeated dialogue appropriate for emergent or developing readers.

First the teacher identifies the repeated spoken phrases from a chosen book and prints each one on a strip of paper. Each child in the group is then given a phrase strip. (If children are arranged in a circle for this activity, their view will be better.) As the teacher rereads the story, he or she pauses when a dialogue phrase is reached and points to the child holding this strip to cue him or her to say the phrase (either by reciting from memory or reading). This continues through the story.

The phrase strips also offer an ideal opportunity to introduce the children to quotation marks and words that describe how speech is uttered (such as "said," "shouted," "asked," or "exclaimed").

Learning about Letters and Sounds

From follow-up activities that focus on comprehension of whole text, sentences, or words, children will also learn a great deal about sounds and letters. This is especially true of language experience exercises, in which children dictate words and help the teacher sound them out while individual letters are printed in sequence. Children will also watch as teachers create Big Books, charts, and other learning materials and may copy words from these exercises. In addition, there are also a number of possible follow-up activities focused exclusively on the letters and their sounds.

Practicing the Alphabet

In traditional approaches to reading instruction, teaching children to recognize the letters of the alphabet is often the first task. More recently, letter recognition has been integrated into reading larger units of text. If the teacher wishes to focus directly on letters but still maintain the overall approach of the shared book experience, alphabet books can be introduced during reading time and can form the basis of a number of follow-up activities.

Once children have been introduced to a fair number of the books, they can, for example, create their own Alphabet Big Book. Each letter of the alphabet requires its own page. The children can work alone or with a partner. Each child or pair is given a letter of the alphabet to develop. The children search through magazines for pictures of objects whose names begin with the target letter. Teachers can give the children hints of things they might find; for example, the child who has the letter "h" can be directed to look for hats, houses, horses, and so on.

The children then create collages with their clippings by pasting them onto durable paper (an old file folder works well). The entire collection of 26 pages (and perhaps one introductory and one concluding page) can be bound together as a Big Book or displayed in the classroom. These letter "posters" can then be used for a number of different activities. For example, the children can each be given one of the letters to hold. (If there are fewer than 26 children in the class, some can manage two letters; if there are more than 26 children, some can be given duplicate letter posters.) For a warm-up exercise teachers can call out different letters and have the child holding that letter stand up. Then the children can be asked to join in with various alphabet songs and jingles.

To reinforce the idea that sounds and letters correspond, one of the letter posters can be selected as the focus for a minilesson on sounds. Children can be asked to call out words that begin with that letter and these words can be written around the border of the letter page.

As children begin to associate sounds with letters, they can play the "trip" game. The children each take a letter poster and arrange themselves in alphabetical order in a circle. "A" starts out by saying "We're going on a trip and we are going to take an apple [or any object beginning with 'a']." "B" then says, "We're going on a trip and we are going to take an apple and a banana," and so on around the circle. If a child can't remember what someone is going to bring, he or she can be reminded so the game can continue and everyone can have a turn.

Contrasting Initial Consonants

No topic in emergent reading has been more hotly debated in recent years than the merits of instruction in phonics. Anderson et al. (1985) state that the goal of phonics instruction is to enable young readers to "use information about the relationship between letters and sounds and letters and meanings to assist in the identification of known words and to independently figure out unfamiliar words" (p. 43). They recommend that phonics be taught at the earliest grade levels and that instruction be kept simple.

In contrast, Manning, Manning, and Kamii (1988) caution educators against undertaking phonics instruction before children have had broad literary experiences. Their study found some kindergartners seemed to become confused by phonics—confused to the point where their progress in reading and writing was impeded.

Holdaway's (1986) recommendations for phonics instruction take both points of view into account: "We never teach the forms of language before or in isolation from the functions, simply because they would not be learned, which is the classic reason for not discretely teaching particular aspects of language" (p. 44). Instruction in phonetic analysis, he argues, should evolve from the stories the children hear and from language in their environment.

The shared book experience provides teachers with many opportunities to present lessons in letter-sound relationships through incidental instruction with individual children and through direct teaching procedures. For example, a teacher can select two letters that have contrasting sounds. The sounds for *t* and *m*, for instance, contrast well; the sounds for *p* and *b* are not very distinct.

When children begin to show an interest in the different sounds, the teacher can select a child or two to go through the text of a Big Book, song, or poem to locate all the words beginning with the target letters. The teacher lists these words on a piece of chart paper. The

Personal Dictionaries

Teaching Idea

F or this activity each child in the class needs a booklet with 26 pages. (If this booklet is held together with paper brads or some other removable fastener, more pages can be added as required.) The booklet should also have front and back covers. At the top of each of the 26 pages write a letter of the alphabet (in order).

The children can use their personal dictionaries in a number of ways to keep track of words beginning with particular letters:

- They can copy the key words from Big Books and other predictable literature onto the correct pages.
- They can write down words they wish to remember.
- They can note names of objects encountered in the classroom, school, or neighborhood.
- They can write down words used in theme units.

To help the children remember the words they include in their dictionaries, encourage them to illustrate their words with small pictures whenever possible. Be sure to give the children opportunities to share their dictionaries with others in the class to compare entries.

children can then suggest other words beginning with the same target sounds to add to the list. If any of the children's names begin with the target letters, they should be added to the list, too. When the chart has 10 to 20 words, the teacher should help the children read over the entire list.

Putting Letters in Sequence

Children get a great deal of practice with letter order whenever they write. Teachers should therefore encourage children to write as often as possible and enlist their help in creating Big Books and related literacy learning materials. To reinforce a lesson on key words, for example, children can make their own sets of key-word cards. The children can simply print the letters on index cards with felt pens or crayons or cut out letters from old newspapers and paste them in sequence onto the index cards. If a word processor is available, children can also be encouraged to input and print key words using this medium. Whichever method is chosen, the resulting cards can be put to good use in many follow-up activities.

A Range of Possibilities

A wide variety of activities appropriate for use as follow-ups to a read-aloud session have been suggested in this chapter. It is up to the teacher to choose and adapt these activities to suit his or her particular situation and the needs and backgrounds of the children in the class. Children living in urban areas, for example, will have different interests and experiences than children growing up in rural areas. As a result,

Pointing to Words

When children are beginning to sort out sounds and letters and are becoming familiar with print, they often guide their reading by pointing to the words on the page. In the past, teachers discouraged pointing, but we now know that it is a beneficial practice that ought to be encouraged and even modeled by teachers when they read aloud from enlarged text.

When a young child looks at an object, he or she regards it from every viewing angle. In contrast, in reading, children must direct their visual attention from left to right and from top to bottom (in English, at least). Many youngsters will benefit greatly from using their fingers to guide their eyes along a line of print.

Clay (1979), in gathering observational records of children during their first years of school, found that all the children went through a finger-pointing stage in their reading development. She also noted that the children naturally gave up using their fingers as their reading speeds and proficiency increased.

two teachers might handle the same predictable book quite differently depending on the children in the class. At-risk readers or second-language learners may need to participate in many teacher-developed and -directed activities for each predictable story to enable them to comprehend its text. With more mature students, the teacher might consider the children's ideas for follow-up activities.

While many of the activities described here require the direction and at-

For this activity you will need a business-size envelope for every key word. Make a shallow pocket to hold the letters in place by folding up an inch or less of the envelope's bottom edge and stapling it at the right and left edges. Print the key words on durable paper, leaving extra space below each word so that it will show above the pocket on the envelope. Cut the individual letters apart. All the letters for one key word are stored in one envelope. The child selects an envelope, takes the letters out, and puts them in the correct sequence in the pocket to spell the key word.

If you use different colored index cards for each word, the children will have an easier time when they use this activity on their own. Spots of matching color can be put on the different envelopes to help the children when they are picking up the letters to put them away.

Teaching Idea

tention of the teacher, others have been designed for children to complete without much adult supervision. As the teacher works with one group of children, a second group can be engaged at the listening center and a third can be working on independent activities.

With the rich, vast collection of predictable literature now available, it is not surprising that there are so many possibilities for follow-up activities, all of which have pedagogical value. Teachers will undoubtedly come up with other ideas to implement in their classrooms.

CHAPTER FOUR

The Writing Connection

In the past, the primary concern of language arts instruction was reading; instruction in writing for very young children invariably meant lessons in penmanship. Thankfully, times have changed and writing is now being emphasized even in the earliest grades.

In recent years, numerous studies have focused on young children's writing capabilities (see, for example, Bakst & Essa, 1990; Calkins, 1986; Fountas & Hannigan, 1989; Hall & Duffy, 1987). Harste, Woodward, and Burke (1984) contend that their data "support the notion that young children are written language users and learners long before they receive formal instruction" (p. 82). Jalongo and Zeigler (1987) found that kindergarten children are frequently more interested in printing their own letters and words than in reading published materials. Graves (1983) says that children entering first grade have more confidence in their writing abilities (about 90 percent of the children in his study said they could write) than in their ability to read (about 15 percent).

It has also become clear that writing is an important complement to reading. Children may well gain more knowledge about letter-sound relationships by attempting to express their ideas in writing than by completing any number of phonics worksheets. Gunderson and Shapiro (1988) observed two groups of first grade children in classrooms that emphasized whole language approaches and writing opportunities. They determined that these children *produced* 18 times the number of words they would have *encountered* in a typical basal series. These researchers reasoned that the numerous writing activities undertaken in these classrooms enabled the children to learn phonics skills as well as rules that govern English spelling. Clay (1979), Teale and Sulzby (1989), and Tovey (1979) all posit that the same behaviors children use in writing are used to organize the behaviors they require for reading. In broad terms, when children see themselves as authors, they bring new insight and understanding to the materials they read. And because they are striving to create meaningful text themselves, they become more determined to seek meaning in the writings of others.

In part because of this increased interest in children's writing and its relationship to reading, many teachers are now responding differently to children's writing than they did in the past. For example, they are accepting children's spelling approximations and have come to realize that being able to spell is not a necessary precursor to being able to write.

When children write words based on their own understandings of letter-sound relationships, the result is "invented spelling." Children appear to go through four stages in their efforts to spell and write. In the first stage, one letter may represent an entire word ("L" indicating *elephant*, for example). In the second stage, the child adds a final phoneme— "ht" would stand for *hat*. Vowel representations are observed in the third stage, although children are often inconsistent in their use of vowels. It is not uncommon at this stage for the same word, used three times in a passage, to be spelled in three different ways. Each word seems to present the child with a unique problem. In the fourth stage, the child begins to use conventional spellings for many words, particularly if he or she has started to read.

Teachers should encourage children's attempts to write and accept their invented spellings in the same way parents accept an infant's efforts to speak. There is no evidence that a child who begins to write by using invented spelling will be retarded in his or her ability to use traditional spelling later on. In fact, when children write frequently without fear of having their errors pointed out, their spelling and penmanship often improve naturally (Calkins, 1986). The children's own writing activities provide them with individualized practice in phonics and spelling that cannot be duplicated by exercises or commercial materials (Sowers, 1982).

The reading activities associated with the shared book experience lead naturally to a variety of writing activities. The rich and enticing diet of literature proffered through many read-aloud sessions is in itself beneficial to children's writing; as Graves (1983, p. 67) notes, "All children need literature. Children who are authors need it even more.... They need to be surrounded with poetry, stories, information books, biography, science, and history—imaginative and factual books. The children need to hear, speak, and read literature." In addition, the many follow-up activities related to read-aloud times provide ample opportunities for writing. Children can work together to create Big Books and other reading materials; when the teacher engages children in language experience and other activities, he or she is demonstrating the links between the spoken and the written language. These sorts of activities provide the groundwork for writing development and encourage children to view writing as a natural mode of expression (Jalongo & Zeigler, 1987).

In this chapter I describe and provide examples of the writing process, suggest general approaches to encourage writing in the classroom, and highlight the connection between predictable literature and the writing experience. Throughout the chapter practical teaching ideas are offered to help link theory with effective classroom practice.

The Writing Process

Many adults approach the task of writing with trepidation. They often harbor memories of unpleasant classroom episodes and the teacher's red pen. Young children, however, do not have such fears. They regard writing simply as an extension of drawing, as a way of expressing themselves: "Just as they fearlessly construct garages, towers, even cities out of a handful of blocks, so, too, they fearlessly write letters, signs, newspapers, and books out of a handful of consonants" (Calkins, 1983, p. 12).

Perhaps the children Calkins is describing put such effort and enthusiasm into their writing because their teachers have altered many of their classroom practices. These teachers probably accept the children's invented spellings; they are probably aware of the stages children go through in learning to write and the processes that all authors use when they write. Indeed, the teaching of writing has undergone fundamental changes since the 1970s. These changes have occurred in part because of studies that have analyzed what proficient writers and readers do as they write and read. In addition, teachers have learned to incorporate ideas and processes used by professional writers into their own literacy teaching.

Several researchers have identified the stages authors move through from the inception of the idea to the finished product. It is important to note, however, that these stages are seldom clear cut and that writers generally move back and forth between them. Graves (1983) reasons: "When a person writes, so many components go into action simultaneously that words fail to portray the real picture" (p. 221).

The first broad stage is prewriting, or "rehearsing." Graves describes some of the activities a writer might undertake at this beginning step: "Rehearsal refers to the preparation for composing and can take the form of daydreaming, sketching, doodling, making lists of words, outlining, reading, conversing, or even writing lines as a foil to further rehearsal" (p. 221). Since young children often perceive writing as an extension of drawing, their drawings frequently serve as rehearsals for the written messages they wish to express. They will often refer to these drawings as they are writing, to help them clarify and remember the thoughts they wish to convey.

Another type of prewriting activity used with young children is a simple read-aloud session with a follow-up time for brainstorming about related ideas for writing projects. According to Nelson (1989), story reading helps children relate themes in the literature to their own experiences. Discussions about stories, a fundamental component of the shared book experience, will often generate ideas for language experience activities, group writing projects, and stories that children write independently.

The writing or composing phase begins when the writer starts work on the actual text. For emergent writers this is a slow, deliberate activity. Children must first have an idea to express; then they must put the idea into words, sound out every word in order, remember which letters are associated with the sounds, and finally remember how to formulate the individual letters. Young children may have to return to the start of their writing each time they finish a word in order to remember what their original idea was and to determine where they are in its expression. Graves (1983) cautions, "Writers of all ages can only focus on so much at a time. Show me a writer who concentrates equally on handwriting, spelling, topic, language, organization, and information and I will show you a confused writer" (p. 241). For a young child to produce any written piece is in itself a considerable achievement and is worthy of praise.

The next phase in the writing process is revising, which encompasses two basic components: rewriting content to ensure that ideas have been expressed so that others can understand them, and correcting mechanical and grammatical errors. With young children it is advisable to work on these two components separately (Slaughter, 1988). When children read their pieces aloud, for example, it is easier to focus exclusively on the clarity of the ideas. Children often make assumptions about the background knowledge of their audience. Because they have had certain experiences in their lives, they assume everyone else understands these experiences from their perspective. As a result, they routinely leave out key bits of information that are vital to an understanding of the total message. The sharing of writing in its formative stages helps children become less egocentric in these thought processes.

Errors such as spelling mistakes are dealt with separately through individual

Predictable literature provides an excellent resource for modeling different writing strategies and skills. This activity shows how you can demonstrate brainstorming to help children generate ideas for their own writing. The description is based on Libby Handy's *Boss for a Week*, a story that seems designed to engage children in some wishful thinking! It is a particularly good book for at-risk readers.

After sharing the book with the class, start off with a prewriting activity. Print "If I were boss for a week, I would..." on the chalkboard. Divide the class into groups of four or five, and ask the groups to talk among themselves about what they would do if they were boss for a week. A member of the group can jot down ideas (invented spelling is acceptable, of course). After five or ten minutes, ask a member of each group to share what they have discussed and use the ideas to create a master list on the chalkboard:

> If I were boss for a week, I would...
> never eat spinach
> leave my room the way it is
> have all the ice cream for myself
> watch what I want on TV
> never have a bath
> stay up late every night

When you have a fair number of suggestions, review the list with the class.

Next, model writing for the children. Create a complete sentence based on one of the suggestions from the brainstormed list: "If I were boss on Monday, everyone else would have to pick up things but my bedroom could be messy."

Then have the children follow your example to create drafts of their own. Always encourage them to come up with new variations and patterns. Meet with the children individually (as necessary) to help them express their ideas as clearly as possible. It is better to point out corrections in spelling, grammar, or punctuation during a second conference.

The children can then illustrate their sentences and share their work with the class. If the children have been particularly productive, you can bind their illustrated sentence pages together into a class book.

conferences between the teacher and the author. The teacher can select one or two problems in one of the child's early drafts as a focus for a minilesson with the child (Clay, 1979).

Of course, not every piece of writing follows this exact process, and not every effort a child makes will result in a product suitable for "publishing" and keeping as reading material for repeated use. (Graves, 1983, suggests that about one in four or five writing attempts might reach the point where it is developed enough to be published.) As with any creative endeavor, however, children need opportunities to experiment, to try new approaches, and to take risks. Teachers are advised to remember Smith's (1982) dictum: A child learns to write by writing.

Classroom Strategies

These days during writing sessions early childhood teachers serve as facilitators, models, and managers during writing sessions, rather than filling the traditional role of resident experts and imparters of knowledge. Classrooms today are considerably more child-centered than in the past; children are now responsible for selecting their own writing topics and assisting one another in a number of ways.

A variety of useful techniques are available to early childhood teachers, and many of them can be easily incorporated into the general approach of the shared book experience. Some of the most popular and successful techniques are the writing workshop, dialogue journals, the author's chair, and various related activities designed to encourage response to literature.

The Writing Workshop

Writing requires times—time to develop ideas and put them on paper; time to confer with others and clarify aspects of what has been written; time to polish, publish, and present. Teachers should set aside blocks of time—an hour or more, two or three days a week—to enable children to develop their potential as writers. This time is dedicated to the writing workshop.

The workshop should follow a consistent structure. Calkins (1983) explains: "When classroom [routines] are always changing, always haphazard, this not only puts teachers into the position of choreographing, it also puts children into the position of waiting for their teachers' changing agendas" (p. 31). In the most common form of writing workshop, the children first gather together for a ten-minute minilesson. Minilessons are organized and directed by the teacher. At the early childhood level, such things as spacing between words, punctuation, story themes, or language patterns are appropriate topics for a minilesson. In every case, the teacher should be guided by the children's demonstrated needs and interests. The minilessons are designed not to dictate what the children will write during the remainder of the workshop, but rather to set a tone for writing and to bring a cohesiveness to the class during the workshop session.

After the minilesson, the children take their writing folders and go off to write. Some children will go to work independently on a story in progress; others will go off to a corner of the room where they can share ideas with a partner. A table is designated for children, alone or in groups, to come to the teacher for advice, or the teacher can move around the room giving assistance as needed. A teacher might simply ask a child how things are going and make a brief comment about the child's drawing or writing. On other occasions, he or she may linger to provide some guidance. A prompt such as "Please tell me more" will help young writers develop from simple to more complex modes of expression, and a question such as "What will happen next in your story?" will help children develop their thoughts (Graves, 1983; Hilliker, 1982). The teacher may also hold longer individual conferences with the children as their writing develops.

At the end of writing workshop time, the class reassembles to hear and re-

When Children Copy

With all of this emphasis on the connections between stories and writing, one or two children may decide simply to copy the text of a favorite story word for word. This behavior may grow out of a desire for attention, particularly if others in the class are receiving praise from the teacher and classmates for having created a marvelous story.

While copying should hardly be encouraged, a wise teacher will often say nothing, trusting that the phase will be short lived. These children may have to observe and participate in many group writing sessions before they venture to create original stories. In any event, the tactile experience children have when they copy a story—sentence by sentence, word by word, letter by slow letter—may provide them with security and advance their understanding of printed language.

spond to the work in progress of two or three of the children or to listen to a piece of writing a child has completed.

Shared book experiences provide valuable reinforcement for writing workshop. The predictable literature shared in read-aloud sessions has a noticeable effect on children's writing. Children will often incorporate themes, phrases, or vocabulary from the stories into their own work. To develop this connection between reading and writing, teachers often devote time to discussing the books that have been read in class. Children should also have a stack of favorite storybooks close at hand for inspiration in their writing (Calkins & Harwayne, 1987). When a child does incorporate elements of a predictable story into his or her writing, the teacher can ask the child to present the piece to the rest of the class to help other children get ideas about using stories to enhance their own writing.

Both the writing workshop and the shared book experience foster collaboration and sharing, but both can also support an individualized approach to learning. Most of the instruction during a writing workshop is individual and occurs when a teacher observes one child's work and uses it as the basis for a direct and timely lesson. The teacher becomes, in effect, a collaborator with each author (Calkins, 1986; Hubbard, 1986), as well as the person responsible for creating an environment in which writing can flourish in the classroom as a whole.

The Author's Chair
Children need to hear the words they have written during writing workshop or other activities, and they need to have

others—preferably their own peers—react to this writing. They need, in effect, to share their work with an audience that will provide them with vital feedback. When teachers and other children show a genuine interest in their work, children gain confidence in their writing abilities (Hansen, 1987).

In many elementary classrooms, a special place is set aside for "the author's chair," where children can share the stories they have written. The designated author (or coauthors) sits on the chair while the rest of the children and the teacher gather around on the floor. After the author has presented the work, the teacher models positive responses, praising the writing, noting the most interesting parts, and asking questions to help clarify aspects of the story. The teacher also solicits opinions and questions from the other children.

A child can sit in the author's chair to present either a finished product or a work in progress. With a finished product, the author makes a formal presentation and receives general feedback. After the presentation, the work can be displayed on a bulletin board (perhaps with a picture of the young author and a biographical paragraph similar to what one might find on a book jacket) or placed in the classroom library for all to read. With a work in progress, the idea is to get specific suggestions. If the author has hit a stumbling block, it is often useful to ask questions of an audience. Friends may be able to think of extensions to the story or find passages that would benefit from additional information. This approach, letting the rest of the children in the class assist the emergent writer, has

been used successfully with children as young as four (Bakst & Essa, 1990).

When the author's chair is a tool used at the revising stage of the writing process, it can be merged effectively with both the shared book experience and the writing workshop. In one class, for example, the teacher read aloud Leila Ward's *I Am Eyes: Ni Macho*, a very simple text describing what a young African child sees on waking up. After the read-aloud sessions, two children got together in a corner of the classroom and decided to use the language pattern from Ward's book to describe their own visit to a playground.

The children produced a draft quickly, and rather than helping them edit their work through a conference, the teacher decided to enlist the assistance of the class. The two children climbed into the author's chair together and read the draft to the group of children gathered around them. This is what happened:

Shari: "Ni macho. I am eyes! I see swings and tall slides. I see tires and teeter-totters. I see bars and ladders. I see ropes and rings. I see sand and grass. Ni macho!" And that's what me and Marie wrote.

Enrico: That's a good story!

Sally: It sounds like a fun playground, but I don't get it about the tires. What can you do on tires?

Teacher: That's a good point, Sally. Shari and Marie,

perhaps you could make a drawing to show how the tires were fastened and how the two of you were able to climb on them.

Max: What's a teeter-totter?

Marie: It's a seesaw.

Max: Why don't you say "see-saw" so everyone will know what you're talking about?

Shari: Okay.

Teacher: These are helpful ideas. Does anyone else have anything to say about the story Marie and Shari are working on?

Tom: I liked the part about the tall slide the best.

This sort of social interaction helps writers develop a sense of audience and inspires them to strive for excellence. Bakst and Essa (1990) maintain that this editing process serves to inform children that their words have worth: "The clear message is that their inner feelings and thoughts are valued and are important to others" (p. 149). As an added benefit, the social nature of the gathering at the author's chair gives all the children an opportunity to think about their own writing, to develop skills, and to recognize the strengths and weaknesses of different stories (Estabrook, 1982; Martinez & Teale, 1987). The skills they develop in helping others with their stories will, in turn, assist them in their own writing.

Dialogue Journals

A dialogue journal is a written conversation between a child and a teacher about topics of interest to each of the participants (Bode, 1989). Unlike writing undertaken in a writing workshop, entries in a dialogue journal remain private.

The teacher sets aside 15 or 20 minutes several times a week for the children to write and draw in their journals. The teacher collects the journals and writes a short response to each child, usually on the same page. No corrections to the child's writing are made; instead, the teacher models correct spelling and grammar in his or her response. If, for example, a child writes "the rdt stre ws a vre good sre" ("the rabbit story was a very good story") in response to John Becker's *Seven Little Rabbits*, the teacher might write, "*Seven Little Rabbits* is one of my favorite stories, too. What did you like most? Please draw me a picture of your favorite part." In this nonthreatening manner, the child receives positive reinforcement of his or her writing efforts and is encouraged to take risks and develop ideas.

Dialogue journals have many benefits. In one class, for example, a child wrote in response to *Seven Little Rabbits*, "My fred hed a rabt an it did" ("My friend had a rabbit and it died"). The teacher responded with "I am very sorry to hear about this, Francis. You and your friend must be very sad. Would you like to write a story about a little rabbit?" Francis was then encouraged to express his thoughts about something that was really bothering him. Writing seems to provide many with a mechanism for working out and coming to grips with difficult situations.

Writing a formal book report is probably too daunting a task for emergent and developing readers and writers. If a formal response is desired, or if you are attempting to assess how children feel about a particular text, a response sheet may be a better way to go.

Response Sheet

Prepare a form similar to that shown below. At first, completing this form can be a class exercise; this will give children a chance to see the sorts of responses you're looking for. Later you can ask children to fill out forms individually when they report on particular books. As the children become more familiar with this activity, you can ask them to describe something about the book in more detail.

Teaching Idea

Book Business

Your name _____

Title of book _____

Author's name _____

Here is a drawing based on the book:

The part of the book I liked the best was _____

_____.

Three interesting words in the book are

_____, _____, and _____.

Responding to Literature

Children can be asked to respond to the stories they read or hear in many ways. The traditional form of response is the book report, but a word of caution is in order here: How many books would people read for pleasure if they had to write book reports on each one? In all likelihood, they would cut back their reading habits dramatically.

Although there are times when such a formal response to literature is appropriate, a number of less formal writing activities will also encourage personal involvement with literature. A show-and-tell session, for example, could be dedicated to sharing books children have enjoyed. Hansen (1987) maintains, "Children learn more about the value of reading when they share a good book with a friend than when they draw circles around words or fill in blanks" (p. 87). These sharing sessions can lead naturally into writing activities in which children comment on the books discussed. They can also create drawings, paintings, collages, or dioramas. When children share literature through talking, drawing, and writing, the stories come alive and become a part of their personal experiences (Stewig & Sebesta, 1989). This will boost children's interest in both reading and writing.

Some Ideas for Getting Started

Writing, like reading, takes practice. Teachers should therefore provide children with frequent opportunities to practice their writing. At the beginning of the school year, writing activities might be whole class efforts, with the teacher modeling the stages and processes a writer uses and the children contributing their ideas. (This is a useful way to start out with at-risk writers, as well.) Later on, children can work on their own or in collaborative groups of two or three.

Teachers should provide writing materials for children in various locations in the classroom, perhaps in special containers. These containers might include a variety of supplies—crayons, pencils, felt pens, scissors, paste, different kinds of paper, envelopes, and magazines. Teachers should also have a

Collaborative Writing

- In the past, children were expected to do most schoolwork by themselves, and cooperation between children was often regarded as cheating. Teachers today are more realistic; they realize that in the "real world," people must cooperate with one another in order to accomplish almost anything. Encouraging cooperation in the classroom helps children prepare for life.

- Children respond well to collaborative activities because these activities foster self-confidence, friendships, and increased learning (Crouse & Davey, 1989). When young writers are encouraged to interact with others, they are better able to generate ideas, clarify their thoughts, and elaborate on the content of their writing (Piazza & Tomlinson, 1985). They will stick to the task longer and will complete the activity with less dependence on the teacher. Rather than "cheating," collaboration is a valuable way to promote learning at all levels.

supply of blank booklets available for the children. These booklets can be very simple—six to ten pieces of scrap paper stapled together—or more elaborate. Odd sizes and shapes appeal to children, as do booklets with decorative covers made from construction paper, old wallpaper samples, or giftwrap. If supplies are handy, children will be able to write whenever inspiration strikes.

Some teachers provide children with models for stories and suggestions for topics; others encourage children to choose their own topics. The activities suggested in this section show how predictable literature can inspire and influence writing projects, but teachers should

71

certainly encourage children to be creative in their endeavors. The descriptions that follow are merely a starting point.

Activities for Emergent Writers

If the teacher has introduced some key words from a predictable text and has created a set of key-word cards, these can be used in a follow-up writing activity. After reading a Big Book to the children, the teacher places key-word cards where they are easily visible (for instance, across the ledge of the chalkboard or spread out on the floor). The class can then work together to compose sentences (and eventually brief stories) using any of these key words. Children can write these sentences in their booklets, copying the key words and using invented spelling for the other words.

Once the children understand the process and have practiced it with the class, they can complete the activity more independently. The teacher should review each of the key words at the outset, and the children should be encouraged to help each other with any problems they may encounter. Later the children can use the key-word cards for other Big Books or their key-word dictionaries for inspiration for other writing projects.

Another activity suitable for individual children or for small groups is the creation of caption books. The teacher can select a theme based on a predictable book that has been read aloud. The theme statement should be written on the first page of each child or group's booklet. The children then draw or cut from magazines pictures that reflect the theme and paste these into their booklets. Using invented spelling, the children label or describe these pictures. Once they add a cover, complete with title and author(s), they can share their book with the rest of the class.

Very young children can also participate in creating more extended text. Predictable literature may influence children to create their own stories by borrowing repetitive patterns from their favorite books. Teachers can encourage this development with a group writing project based on a highly patterned book, such as Bill Martin Jr's *Brown Bear, Brown Bear, What Do You See?* Children can be given sheets with the repeated phrases reproduced and be asked to supply new text for the missing

Books and Themes

- These predictable books suggest themes appropriate for caption books.
- Margaret Wise Brown's *The Friendly Book*: I like...
- John Burningham's *Mr. Gumpy's Motor Car*: things that go fast
- E.B. Chance's *Just in Time for the King's Birthday*: presents I would give the president [prime minister, queen, etc.]
- Pat Hutchins's *The Surprise Party*: things I would like to have at my party
- Ruth Krauss's *The Carrot Seed*: things that grow
- Anita Lobel's *The Pancake*: I like to eat...
- Mercer Mayer's *There's a Nightmare in My Closet*: scary things
- Christina Rossetti's *What Is Pink?*: What is red [yellow, green, etc.]?
- Shel Silverstein's *A Giraffe and a Half*: very tall things
- Charlotte Zolotow's *Some Things Go Together*: these things go together

Familiar, traditional children's stories can inspire children to work together to create their own story. This activity uses a language experience approach to produce a class story. Even though the children won't be doing any of the *physical* writing, they will still be authors because they will provide the ideas.

Ask the children how they could make a familiar story— "Henny Penny" is an appropriate choice—more personal, perhaps by giving it another setting and different characters. You might suggest, for example, that children in the class become the main characters: Billy Willy, Newsy Suzie, and Chasin' Jason could replace Turkey Lurkey, Ducky Lucky, and Foxy Loxy. (Let the children suggest the variations for their own names to avoid the possibility of embarrassment.) You can also change the story's setting from the farmyard to the classroom.

The new story might begin this way:

> Once upon a time, when Billy Willy was reading quietly at his desk, a piece of paper fell on his head. "The ceiling is falling, the ceiling is falling! I am going to tell the principal!"
>
> So he went along until he met Newsy Suzie. "The ceiling is falling and I am going to tell the principal," said Billy Willy.
>
> "May I go with you?" asked Newsy Suzie....

And so the story continues, with the phrases "The ceiling is falling" and "I am going to tell the principal" repeated over and over.

Try not to put too many ideas into the children's heads; the story should be their own. Just get an idea started and then let the children's imaginations take over.

If you have access to a personal computer, it will be faster for you to enter the children's words directly on a word-processing program. On another day, editing the text will be an excellent group lesson in revising a story for clarity and correctness. The computer will also make it easy for you to provide each child with printed copies of the drafts and the finished story.

When everyone is happy with the story, let the children decide on a title. Then they can illustrate the pages and prepare the front and back covers, listing the whole group as both authors and illustrators.

words ("Pink giraffe in a hat, what do you see?" for example).

Once the children are comfortable with the activity, teachers should encourage them to depart from the formula as much as they'd like. A child might want to create a "What Do You Hear?" story after listening to *Brown Bear*, for example. When one child comes up with a unique perspective or slant, some praise from the teacher will usually start a trend in this direction.

One word of warning: Wason-Ellam (1988) cautions against using too much of the "formula" type of writing. She reasons that if carried to extremes, these activities may come to resemble fill-in-the-blank workbook exercises that can actually inhibit children's writing. Teachers may want to intersperse emergent writing activities with a few oral exercises and then, as soon as the children are ready, move them into more creative projects.

Activities for Developing Writers

Once young children have had some initial experiences with writing, they will be eager to experiment on their own. One technique that allows considerable creative freedom but still provides some necessary structure is to suggest using the title, an introductory passage, or a phrase from a favorite book as the starting point for a new story. Children might invent an entirely new story called *Good-Night, Moon* or adapt Beatrice Schenk de Regniers's *May I Bring a Friend?* to describe who they'd bring along to dinner at the prime minister's house.

If all the children are working from the same starting point, it will be interesting to compare their finished products. The children's writing and any artwork they produce to accompany it might make an attractive bulletin board display.

The same sort of activity can be cast as a group project to good effect because collaborating on stories gives developing writers some support. Teachers can suggest a variation on a theme from a favorite book and then ask groups of six to eight children to come up with a new story. Beatrice Schenk de Regniers and Beni Montresor's *Willy O'Dwyer Jumped in the Fire* might, for instance,

Shape Books

- Many children's stories are ideal for inspiring "shape books," homemade books shaped like a character or object from a story. These books appeal greatly to young children. The only restriction in selecting a children's book for this idea is that the main object or creature in the story should be fairly chunky and easily recognizable in outline form. Children might, for example, make an owl-shaped book inspired by Pat Hutchins's *Good-Night, Owl!* or a house-shape book based on Joanna Cole's *This Is the Place for Me.*

- To make a shape book, first project an outline of the chosen shape onto a sheet of durable paper, such as a discarded file folder. Trace around the outline and cut out the shape to create a template to use in tracing the shape onto construction and scrap paper for the covers and interiors of the shape books. Then staple the books in an inconspicuous spot.

- Encourage children to draw and write in their books about anything the shape inspires, using either the predictable story or their imaginations as the starting point.

lead one group to develop a new story that begins "Tommy MacFuddle jumped in a puddle. The puddle was so deep, he hopped in a jeep. The jeep went so fast, he crashed into a sheep...."

The stories do not have to make sense; children should be encouraged to take liberties with logic and to have fun. The group can work together to come up with the entire text or each member can contribute a line based on the one before. Each group can then illustrate its story and present it to the class.

Predictable literature offers endless inspiration for writing activities of this type. For example, John Burningham's *Come away from the Water, Shirley* might lead to a new book called *Don't Climb the Tree, Peter*, Eric Carle's *Have You Seen My Cat?* might inspire a story about finding a lost dog, pencil, or mitten; and Maurice Sendak's *Chicken Soup with Rice* might form the basis for a book patterned on the joys of peanut butter and jam. Once children have had a fair amount of writing experience of this sort, they will probably begin to use predictable stories in many individual ways to inspire their own creations.

When young authors have demonstrated that they are ready for a higher degree of independence in their writing, teachers can still use published books to guide them. Children and adults alike often find certain aspects of a book appealing or thought-provoking. During the discussions that follow a read-aloud session, children will frequently bring up an interesting facet of the story or ask questions about an issue raised in the book. Some of the best ideas for writing activities come up in such dis-

cussions. To encourage this sort of thinking, teachers can ask the children what they enjoyed about the story or whether there is anything about the story they might want to bring into their own writing. John Tarlton's *Going to Grandma's*, for example, might suggest a few ideas for writing about grandparents; John Burningham's *Mr. Gumpy's Outing* raises questions about friendship that some children might like to explore.

Publishing and Presenting

When a child creates a written work that he or she is particularly pleased with, it should be published or displayed. Making a child's work public is an excellent way to boost self-confidence; it tells the child that his or her efforts have merit and are appreciated. The author's chair gives children an opportunity to share their work orally with their classmates, but children's creations should also be available for viewing. They can either be displayed on the walls of the classroom or school corridors or published as homemade books and kept in a special place in the classroom library. Emergent readers often choose to read books by their classmates—after all, if there is a word or an idea they do not understand, they can always ask the author. (This then becomes a shared book experience of another sort!)

Occasionally children might like to share their best creations with an audience wider than their own classmates. Other people can then be asked to come into the classroom for a special presentation. Parents of the children in the class can be invited, as can children from other classes; the school principal is often an eager and appreciative audience member. Stories created by the children can also be presented during open houses and other meetings to which parents are invited. An ambitious teacher may want to organize a special "authors' night" to celebrate young writers.

Reading Books, Writing Stories

Although the shared book experience does not lead directly to writing activities, the literature used in this approach can inspire a great deal of creativity. Literature in general has an enormous and positive impact on the writing of young children. Children's creativity and sensitivity to language are nurtured when they hear and read stories (Kintisch, 1986; Stewig & Sebesta, 1989). Fountas and Hannigan (1989) contend:

> Rich literature experiences enable developing writers to analyze how the finest authors engage in their craft. As they read the works of good writers, they internalize new language techniques that may be applied to their own writing. As they write, they realize the challenge of creating text that will successfully communicate their ideas to their readers. A classroom with a variety of interesting language opportunities inspires students to move from reading to writing and writing to reading and thus experience this fundamental connection (p. 136).

Sharing many outstanding trade books with young children clearly provides them with a good grounding when they begin to explore writing.

CHAPTER FIVE

Across the Curriculum

The phrase "reading across the curriculum" suggests that procedures, activities, and materials appropriate for language learning can be used in other subject areas as well. Sebesta (1989) observes that when teachers use children's literature in content areas other than reading, students become more curious about the topic: "Trade books serendipitous to a curricular topic can make the difference between a passive reader who quits when the bell rings and an active, lifelong, self-motivated reader/learner" (p. 114).

The benefits of integrating literature across the curriculum are, in fact, two-way—other areas of study complement and reinforce instruction in language arts. Learning about different systems of communication (art, mathematics, or music, for example) enables students to view information from different perspectives. Harste, Woodward, and Burke (1984) reason, "In the final analysis, the goal of the language arts program involves expansion of the child's communication potential. Activities which involve other than linguistic ways of knowing should be an integral and natural part of the language arts curriculum" (p. 209). An emphasis on literature across the curriculum also produces an enriched environment for the development of literacy. Strickland and Morrow (1990) suggest that when literacy is integrated with other subjects through theme units, children become aware of reasons for acquiring the ability to read and write, which boosts motivation. And Dillon (1990) contends that when children use the different forms of language to understand new concepts in the subject areas, they are also developing their literacy-related skills.

Reading aloud from predictable literature can obviously lead to learning in areas other than literacy. In fact, for teachers who follow prescribed language arts programs, shared book experiences may be introduced through other subjects to give children the benefits of these language and literature experiences while expanding their knowledge in a particular subject area. In this chapter I provide examples of ways to use predictable literature to teach art, music, mathematics, science, and social studies—all major components of the early childhood curriculum.

Art

Many of the activities described earlier in this book involve artwork of some kind. When the class creates a Big Book, for example, the teacher often prints the text and the children create the illustrations. The major difficulty in integrating the shared book experience with lessons in art lies in dissuading children from copying the usually attractive illustrations directly from predictable books. One way to avoid this problem is to put aside the storybook (or even hide it, if necessary) when the children are creating illustrations. Another way to encourage originality is to use predictable literature as the inspiration for a range of different types of activities. Children can create entirely new Big Books full of original artwork, respond to literature with art projects, or use the work of published illustrators and artists as inspiration for creating with certain techniques.

Predictable stories can spark many responses in the form of art projects. Crayon is a popular medium, but children should also be encouraged to explore other techniques. For example, Plasticine, Play-Doh, or some other form of children's modeling clay is found in most early childhood classrooms. Children can use this medium to create three-dimensional objects and characters—or more elaborate recreations of entire scenes—from the stories they hear or read.

For a particularly popular book, the class may want to try creating a mural. Because of their size, murals are best un-

Making Color Big Books

Teaching Idea

Here's a simple activity to use with very young children who are learning about both literacy and colors. Read a predictable story aloud, and then ask the children to think of objects in the story that are a particular color—green, for example. List all the objects the children come up with, and then ask each child to create a picture of one of them. Each picture is then cut out, labeled, and pasted on a Big Book page. The teacher can fasten several of these pages together to make a collection called *The Big Book of Green Things.*

A slightly more ambitious undertaking is the creation of *The Big Book of Mixed-Up Colors.* Let the children have opportunities to experiment with mixing primary colors and creating pictures from the colors they come up with. One of the easiest ways to do this is to give each child a small amount of paint in only two primary colors. (When they are given all three, children tend to mix them together and wind up with disappointing shades of brown.) Children can experiment mixing a range of shades by using different amounts of their primary colors and then use these shades to create paintings of different objects. When the children have completed their artwork, ask them to tell you about the creations or write down their own thoughts about their works of art. These paintings and descriptions can be fastened together and placed in the class library.

dertaken as a collaboration. Unless the classroom is very large, it is easiest to divide the class into two or three groups and let one group at a time work on the mural. A long strip of brown packing paper about 18 inches (45 cm) wide makes an ideal (and inexpensive) surface for the artwork.

First the children should meet to plan their project, select the parts of the story they wish to include, discuss how they are going to use the strip of paper, and decide who will work on which parts of the mural. This planning step is conceptually similar to the prewriting stage of the writing process. For a successful outcome, it is crucial.

Two techniques for creating murals are particularly successful: crayon resist and collage on a painted background. To make a crayon resist, the children use crayon to draw the characters and objects on the mural paper but they do not color in the background. They should press quite heavily when they draw so that each character or feature is well coated with the crayon wax. The teacher then prepares a wash with diluted pow-

Salt-flour play dough is a popular and durable alternative to Plasticine. It is easy to make and can be stored in air-tight containers until ready to use. Here's the recipe:

Mix 2 cups flour, ½ cup salt, and enough powdered paint to turn the dough a rich color (this is optional, but will make the dough more attractive and fun to use). Sprinkle with ½ tablespoon vegetable oil. Knead in just enough water to make a thick dough.

If children want a permanent sculpture, the shaped dough can be left out to dry in the air or be baked at 300 degrees until hard. The sculpture can be painted or decorated after it has dried.

oped with the addition of details such as clouds (cotton balls) or characters' hair (colored yarn).

Predictable literature can inspire art in another way. Although children should not be encouraged to copy illustrations directly from books, they can certainly use the artwork in children's literature to inspire experimentation with different materials and techniques. In many predictable books, the artwork is unusual in form as well as being exceptionally good. Children thoroughly enjoy trying out different kinds of media and procedures, such as finger painting, collage, chalk, torn tissue paper, border decorations, and print making.

Eric Carle's books, for example, are popular with young children in part because of the charming creatures and objects he depicts. Finger painting provides an easy way for children to create simple animal shapes similar to those in many of Carle's illustrations. Children can use commercially prepared finger paints or liquid starch mixed with dry powdered paint and water. Very young children find it easiest to create large, free-form designs and blocks of color with the paint. When the paint has dried thoroughly, they can then draw an outline of an animal or other object on the surface of the painting, cut it out, and paste it on the page of a class Big Book. Details such as eyes or hair can be drawn in with crayons or felt markers.

Many artists use collage techniques for their illustrations in children's books. In the classic *The Snowy Day*, for example, Ezra Jack Keats seems to have used a variety of cut and torn paper, as well as checkered material for the mother's dress,

dered paint. When the children stroke the paint lightly across the surface with brushes, it will bead away from the crayon drawings and adhere only to the background. One color or wash can be used, or two or more colors can be prepared—one for the sky and another for the ground cover, for example. The wash has the effect of pulling together all the different characters and objects in the mural and creating a more cohesive, attractive product.

To make a collage mural, children work on the background first. They may choose to paint the ground and sky in different colors, or they can create one overall background using sponges to apply the paint. Characters and objects are cut from a variety of materials (corrugated cardboard, giftwrap, wallpaper, and so on) and pasted on the mural paper. The scene can be further devel-

Edith Newlin Chase and Barbara Reid's *The New Baby Calf* is a quiet story about the birth and development of a calf. The text is simple and predictable, making it an ideal selection for emergent readers working on a unit on farm life or animals. The illustrations, created with modeling clay, will appeal to readers at all levels and can inspire many interesting art projects.

Plasticine Relief Pictures

First read the story to the children and then talk about the illustrations. These are relief pictures with Plasticine objects built up on a flat surface to create a sculptured, three-dimensional effect. See if any of the children can guess how the pictures were made. Ask them to speculate about how details such as marks on the grass were done.

Teaching Idea

Now set the children to work on their own relief pictures, based on *The New Baby Calf* or on something from their own imaginations. Give them different colors of Plasticine and the tools they might want to use (such as a rolling pin, fork, spoon, or knife) to create details and texture. Each child will need a piece of cardboard for the background, which can be painted or crayoned in a variety of colors.

wisps of cotton for the clouds, and patterned wallpaper for Peter's pajamas. Any material that can be cut and glued onto paper can be used for collages. Children can try using some of the following:

- wallpaper (from discarded sample books) and giftwrap
- cloth (although it can be difficult to cut with children's scissors)
- sponges (thin enough to cut)
- cotton balls or batting
- newspaper and magazine scraps
- plastic wrap and aluminum foil (flat or crumpled)
- computer paper (printed with overall patterns)

- string, yarn, drinking straws (whole or cut), rubber bands, and paper clips
- doilies, tissues, and paper napkins (plain or patterned)
- colored tissue paper (flat or crumpled)
- corrugated cardboard and Styrofoam
- rubbed paper (newsprint placed on a rough surface and rubbed with crayon)
- leaves, twigs, and grasses

(Note that children should draw objects on the back of wallpaper or giftwrap, so that the outlines can be easily changed or erased and won't be visible when the object is cut out and pasted down with the patterned side showing.)

Pastels and colored chalks are another favorite medium for artists. If the art paper is wiped first with a damp sponge, the chalk will be less messy. For an interesting variation, have the children try using chalk on dark tones of construction paper. The paper mutes the chalk colors, and the effect of light shades on a dark background is most attractive. Hair spray or pastel fixative can be used to keep the finished product from smearing.

Patricia Mullins used colored tissue paper for her beautiful illustrations in Mem Fox's *Hattie and the Fox*. Children can also obtain interesting effects when they create pictures with torn or cut tissue paper; for instance, when one piece of tissue overlaps a piece of a different color, a new shade emerges. Crayon or pen can be used to add finishing details such as facial features.

Children can also try their hands at print making, a technique used by many artists (including Leo Lionni in his delightful book *Swimmy*). Since this can be a messy process, only a few children at a time should work at a table set up for printing. The "ink" for the printing is powdered paint, mixed with water to a fairly thick consistency. (Flat Styrofoam meat trays make ideal containers for the paints.) The children can look around for all sorts of objects to dip into the paint trays to create block prints. Pieces of onion, potato, and carrot work well, as does corrugated cardboard. Children can also cut sponges (ideal because they can be washed and reused) in different shapes and sizes. Since they can do this sort of printing very quickly, children will want to try several different creations, so it's best to supply inexpensive paper such as sheets of newsprint. If the illustrations are to be used for a class Big Book, they can be cut out and glued onto the pages.

A different approach is to ask children to decorate the borders of a Big Book page. In this case, the teacher should first print the text in the middle of the page and then have one or two children create artwork around the print. Simple drawings in crayon or pencil are probably most effective, but children can use any technique to good effect. A fine example of border decoration can be found in Anita Lobel's illustrations for Arnold Lobel's *A Treeful of Pigs*.

Music

Music is an integral part of the curriculum in the early grades. Most children enjoy listening to and making music; in addition, singing songs introduces them to new words and concepts, increases their attention spans, and improves their listening skills (Eliason & Jenkins, 1986; Goodman, 1987). The shared book experience is very compatible and easily integrated with music; indeed, a number of the predictable stories now available in Big Book format were originally known as children's songs. Conversely, many nursery rhymes have been set to music.

These songs have simple melodies and short, predictable verses, which make them ideal for language learning. Overhead transparencies are an excellent vehicle for putting these familiar

The predictable books listed below are just a few of those that are based on songs. Although not all of them are available as Big Books, they can still be shared with young children in a variety of ways.

Hush Little Baby (Aliki)

I Know an Old Lady (Rose Bonne and Abner Garboff)

Over in the Meadow (John Langstaff and Feodor Rojankovsky)

Frog Went A-Courtin' (John Langstaff and Feodor Rojankovsky)

The Fox Went Out on a Chilly Night (Peter Spier)

Mommy, Buy Me a China Doll (Harve Zemach and Margot Zemach)

rhymes to good use in the classroom since they allow the entire class to see all the words clearly. (Longer texts can be printed on story scrolls.) As children sing along, the teacher or a child can point to each word. Since many of the children will be familiar with the rhymes, they can attend to the written text and will soon come to make associations between the words they have memorized and the same words in print. Transparencies and story scrolls are both useful for a variety of follow-up activities. These texts can be particularly effective for helping children recognize rhyming words and spelling patterns.

Another way to link reading and music presents itself when new songs are introduced—a frequent occurrence in the typical early childhood classroom. The teacher can sing the new song to model the tune and words and then show the children the lyrics in enlarged form. The children can then see the text and hear the words at the same time. Hearing and seeing lyrics together can help children learn new songs rapidly and easily. As reinforcement, the teacher can pass out copies of the words to each child. Children can keep these lyrics in folders or paste them into booklets. To help children remember the words, the teacher can have them draw descriptive pictures around the edges of the song sheets.

Many popular recordings are packaged with printed lyrics. These sheets can be laminated or stapled onto cardboard for durability. The lyrics and the accompanying records, tapes, or CDs can then be put in the listening center. Children can listen to the songs and follow along with the words independently. This technique is especially appealing for at-risk readers.

Mathematics

Children find it easier to comprehend elementary concepts regarding numbers, time, and measurement when these concepts are linked to everyday experiences (Maxim, 1984). Predictable stories can be used to connect math to other areas of the curriculum, thus making the lesson more relevant to the child. In addition, many predictable stories make direct references to mathematical concepts and provide illustrations to explain them.

The concept of number is obviously fundamental to mathematics. Although children encounter numbers early in their lives ("No, you can't have five chocolate chip cookies for breakfast," or

The traditional counting song "One Elephant Went Out to Play" can be transformed into a Big Book to help young children learn about counting and one-to-one correspondence—and, in the process, to link reading, music, art, and math. This ridiculous and charming song tells about an elephant who has such enormous fun playing on a spider web that he asks another one to join him; then the two ask another; and so on. By the end, ten elephants are frolicking on the fragile web.

A Big Counting Book

Teaching Idea

First the children will have to get busy and create elephants—55 for the inside of the book and a few extra for the front cover and title page. Each child can come up with his or her own idea for an elephant; you can provide an assortment of paper (plain or patterned wallpaper, aluminum foil, and anything else you think might be appropriate). The elephants will be overlapping on most of the pages, so different colors, patterns, and textures are required to distinguish them.

Print the verses on the left-hand pages and draw the spider webs opposite, as in the illustration below. The children then glue the appropriate number of elephants on each web. Have them create a cover and title page for the Big Book before stapling the pages together and placing the completed work in the class library.

Two Pages, Ready for Elephants

Eight elephants
went out to play,
on a spider's web
one day.

They had such
enormous fun,
they asked another
elephant to come.

The above excerpt is taken from "The Elephants," published in *Singing with Children* (2nd edition, copyright 1970) by Robert Nye, Vernice Nye, Neva Aubin, and George Kyme. Reproduced by permission of the publisher, Wadsworth Publishing Co.

simply "one, two, buckle my shoe"), this does not necessarily mean that they consistently understand what any of these numbers actually represent. Many popular children's books focus directly on numbers and counting; these books can help reinforce early instruction in math. John Becker's *Seven Little Rabbits*, Pat Hutchins's *The Doorbell Rang*, Leo Lionni's *Swimmy*, Bill Martin Jr's *Ten Little Caterpillars*, and David M. Schwartz's *How Much Is a Million?* are a few of the many available to use when introducing numbers and basic arithmetical concepts.

Learning to tell time is another math-related topic often tackled in early childhood classrooms. Katz (1983) reminds educators that "the notion of time can be difficult for children to grasp because it involves measuring something that can't be seen or touched" (p. 9). A number of children's books that relate to time can be shared in read-aloud sessions. Eric Carle's *The Grouchy Ladybug*, for example, features the hours of the day, and the protagonist of his *The Very Hungry Caterpillar* munches its way through the days of the week. Uri Shulevitz's *One Monday Morning* is another good choice for a lesson on the week. For a predictable story that refers to the months of the year, try Maurice Sendak's classic *Chicken Soup with Rice*.

Teachers can invite the children to think of ways of incorporating aspects of time into the stories they write. When a child follows up on this suggestion, his or her story should be brought to the attention of the rest of the class. The children could also work together to create a "Monday to Friday" Big Book in which they describe classroom activities that go on at certain times on certain days.

Another concept that is difficult for young children is the visual display of information in graphs. Achievement test scores indicate that many children struggle to understand information presented in this format if they have not received instruction about it (Slaughter, 1983). One of the most effective ways to help children with this concept is to involve them in the creation of graphs.

Many children's stories can prompt questions whose answers can be graphed. After reading Polly Greenberg's *Oh Lord, I Wish I Was a Buzzard*, for example, the teacher can ask children if they have ever been so hot and tired that they wished they were something else. E.B. Chance's *Just in Time for the King's Birthday* can lead to a poll about what the children would give a king on his birthday. Each child should respond to the question on a small square of paper, either drawing an object or writing its name. The teacher can then prepare a poster with axes to display the results in a bar graph.

To complete the graph, one child attaches his or her square at the bottom of the first column. Then all the other children who have depicted the same type of object staple or pin their squares in that column. When a new object appears, it forms the beginning of a new column. When the graph is finished, the teacher can show the children how easy it is to determine which is the most popular answer to the question.

Figure 4 on the next page shows a partially completed graph based on

Figure 4
Graphing a Wish

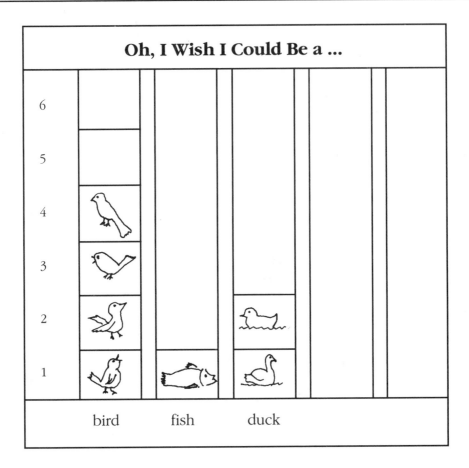

Greenberg's *Oh Lord, I Wish I Was a Buzzard*.

Science

In its broadest sense, science is "asking questions, searching for answers, exploring, experimenting, and perceiving. Science can teach patience and persistence, inquiry, open-mindedness, respect for honest evidence, resourcefulness, self-reliance, and respect for other people's opinions" (Holt et al., 1983, p. 6). The shared book experience can help young children comprehend specific science topics while showing them the relevance of science to their daily lives.

Science involves observing, investigating, analyzing, classifying, comparing, and predicting. Sara E. Barchas's *I Was Walking Down the Road*, a story about a young girl who finds all kinds of interesting creatures as she walks around her neighborhood, can serve as the inspiration for an activity to help children develop skills in these areas.

After reading the story, make plans with the children for a field trip to the schoolyard or some other nearby location. The children can speculate on the kinds of things they might find. The girl in *I Was Walking Down the Road* found animals, but near school the children will more likely find objects and plants. When you return to the classroom, children can compare and discuss what they found. Then give each child a piece of cardboard on which to mount his or her collection of found objects (or drawings of them). The children should make labels or descriptions for the objects they have found. Attach the pieces of cardboard with strips of tape. The accordion book *We Were Walking Around Our School* can be displayed on a long counter or on the window ledge.

Finding Out about the World

Teaching Idea

One science theme that plays an important role in a number of predictable literature selections is the weather. Stories such as Ezra Jack Keats's *The Snowy Day* and Alvin Tresselt's *The Mitten* are very appropriate for any study about winter. *Mushrooms in the Rain* (Mirra Ginsburg) and *One Monday Morning* (Uri Shulevitz) are ideal stories to read on rainy days. Lucinda McQueen's *The Little Red Hen* would be appropriate in either spring or fall. A summer holiday is the setting for John Burningham's *Come away from the Water, Shirley*, and on a sweltering day, the children could all empathize with the main character in Polly Greenberg's *Oh Lord, I Wish I Was a Buzzard*.

Many poems and nursery rhymes also focus on the weather and the seasons. *Poems Children Will Sit Still For* (compiled by de Regniers, Moore, and White) includes 24 poems about weather, all appropriate for young children. A selection of these poems could be printed on overhead transparencies, posters, or chart paper and read to the class. If children decorate the borders with appropriate pictures, posters particularly can make attractive wall displays.

Watching plants grow from seeds they have tended is a popular and exciting activity for children in the early elementary grades. A number of predictable stories can be used to introduce this topic in the classroom; Janina Domanska's

The Best of the Bargain and *The Turnip*, Polly Greenberg's *Oh Lord, I Wish I Was a Buzzard*, Ruth Krauss's *The Carrot Seed*, Alexei Tolstoy's *The Great Big Enormous Turnip*, and different versions of "Jack and the Beanstalk" would all be suitable to read aloud before having children plant their own seeds.

After a read-aloud session and an introductory lesson about growing things, the teacher should divide the class into small groups. Each group will need a number of things to create a miniature garden: seeds (carrot, bean, or flower seeds, for example); planting containers (trimmed-down milk cartons work well); trays; soil; spoons; a watering can; strips of paper; and a date stamp. Children may need advice when they are ready to plant their seeds.

To link this activity to writing, each group can record daily observations in a special book. The children can begin by stamping the date on the first page and describing, in words and pictures, how the seeds were planted. Every day thereafter, the group should get together, observe any changes, tend the garden, and record details in the booklet. When a plant emerges the children can hold a strip of paper next to the plant and mark its height. This strip can be pasted into the booklet, and new strips can be added each day to show the plant's growth—a good link to math.

As the plants develop, children can refer to their booklets to create a Big Book called *A Seed Grows Up*. Here they can recall how they planted their seeds, how they cared for them, how long they had to wait for the seeds to germinate, and how the plant developed. Their comments should be fairly short and to the point. The teacher can help them record each idea on the page that will be used for the Big Book and select children to draw appropriate pictures for each page and the cover.

Animals, of course, make frequent appearances in children's literature. Many youngsters spend hours poring through animal books, fact and fiction, even when they are able to read few of the words. Animal characters play a prominent role in a majority of predictable books; teachers can use this feature to good advantage in many science-related activities.

The study of animals provides an ideal opportunity to introduce children to the notion of making comparisons. A number of predictable books have more than one animal character and can therefore be used to help children learn about animals' similarities and differences. Joan M. Lexau's *Crocodile and Hen*, for example, makes fairly direct comparisons between those two animals; Mem Fox's *Hattie and the Fox* reveals characteristics of seven animals. John Burningham's *Mr. Gumpy's Motor Car*, Marjorie Flack's *Ask Mr. Bear*, Mercer Mayer's *What Do You Do with a Kangaroo?*, John Tarlton's *Have You Ever Seen?*, Alvin Tresselt's *The Mitten*, and Margot Zemach's *It Could Always Be Worse* are just a few other children's books that can be used to compare animals.

Any of these books can be read aloud, and children can be asked to describe all the differences between the animals depicted. (Children should be encouraged to use the book's illustra-

Figure 5
Chart of Animal Characteristics

The Animals in *Hattie and the Fox*					
	skin cover	number of legs	what they eat	how they give birth	how they move
hen					
fox					
goose					
pig					
sheep					
horse					
cow					

tions and their own background knowledge here.) Each statement they make can be listed under a category heading in a comparison chart similar to that shown in Figure 5. The same procedure can be used to come up with similarities.

The teacher can suggest some of the categories for comparison; the children can suggest others. If there are many animals to compare, there should be fewer categories for the children to consider. The chart shown in Figure 5, for instance, probably has too many categories for very young children.

To link writing and the study of animals, children can work in pairs to help each other with ideas for a Big Book of animal riddles. Animals are good subjects for riddles, and children (particularly at-risk readers) respond enthusiastically to this sort of activity. The children simply print the question ("What animal carries his house around on his back?" for example) on one side of a large sheet of paper and the answer ("a turtle"), possibly with a drawing, on the back of the page.

Social Studies

The social studies curriculum at the early childhood level is usually quite diverse, focusing on areas such as self, the family, the community, and people from other cultures. It also often includes units about important aspects of day-to-day life, such as travel and housing needs. Lessons on these topics present teachers with ideal opportunities to introduce nonfiction literature as well as relevant fiction. Although emergent readers will not be able to read much of the text themselves, they can learn a great deal from the pictures and read-aloud sessions; developing readers will be able to read many of the books discussed in this section on their own. Children frequently develop lasting interests in specific topics through such explorations.

Self and Others

Many children's books describe a multitude of emotions. By reading these stories in class, teachers help children understand some of their own feelings. Wells (1986) reasons that stories help children make sense of their lives, enabling them to make connections among various events. This understanding, in turn, can improve children's self-image, as well as the way they relate to family members, friends, and other people.

Discussing a book after it has been read aloud can promote a deeper understanding of the story, its characters, and the emotions and situations it describes. Mercer Mayer's *There's a Nightmare in My Closet*, for example, is an ideal vehicle for encouraging children to express their fears. After reading the story, the teacher can initiate a discussion about nightmares and other scary things. When children express their fears, they soon

come to realize that others in the class have similar feelings. The teacher can also ask the children to share ways of coping with their fears. Other children's stories raise different topics for discussion. Maurice Sendak's *Where the Wild Things Are*, for example, can lead to a talk about anger; Robyn Supraner's *Would You Rather Be a Tiger?* highlights the demands that adults make on children; and Eric Carle's *The Mixed-Up Chameleon* or Mirra Ginsburg's *The Chick and the Duckling* can encourage children to talk about the feelings they have about themselves.

Teachers can choose from a wide selection of predictable books to use in helping children learn about interpersonal relationships. They can, for instance, initiate a discussion about sticking by friends and family after reading Susan Blair's version of *Three Billy Goats Gruff*, while Janina Domanska's *The Turnip* might inspire a talk about helping other people; Alvin Tresselt's *The Mitten* could help children understand the importance of getting along with others; and Margot Zemach's *It Could Always Be Worse* will be valuable to children living in crowded conditions.

Of course, many children's stories deal with family relationships and concerns. A number of stories—from the traditional (like "Little Red Riding Hood") to the classic (P.D. Eastman's *Are You My Mother?* or Ezra Jack Keats's *Over in the Meadow*) to the more modern (Leo Lionni's *The Biggest House in the World* or Mercer Mayer's *Me Too!*)—can be used in the early childhood classroom to help children learn how different fami-

If children are reluctant to talk about their feelings, try role playing. This activity provides a nonthreatening framework in which to explore issues raised in a story while providing a good opportunity for active involvement in literature.

Any predictable story with a number of major characters is suitable. Marjorie Flack's classic *Ask Mr. Bear*, for example, could involve eight children in role playing.

Read the story over once. Then ask for volunteers to play the parts—for *Ask Mr. Bear* you'll need someone for Danny, Mrs. Hen, Mrs. Goose, Mrs. Goat, Mrs. Sheep, Mrs. Cow, Mr. Bear, and Mother. Parts can be adjusted to provide balance—you may want to replace Mrs. Goose with Mr. Gander, for example.

Now reread the story pausing for the players to supply dialogue appropriate for their characters. They don't need to parrot the exact words from the book; in fact, ad libbing should be encouraged. Soon some of the children, while still "in character," will provide dialogue about their own feelings on the issues raised in the story. This will also help them begin to understand the nature of point of view in literature.

Teaching Idea

---

lies work. Teachers should read widely from these types of books to provide children with a broad picture of family life and human relationships.

There are also a number of children's books available that can serve as a springboard for learning about people beyond the confines of family and immediate community. Many countries comprise diverse groups of people, each group with its own distinctive cultural identity and traditions. Literature can help children identify the common emotions, needs, and desires of people throughout the world and also realize and appreciate different people's unique attributes (Bishop, 1987).

Anthologies of folktales from different cultural groups are readily available from libraries. (Bibliographic information for some of these collections can be found in the appendix. In addition, Gillespie and Gilbert's *Best Books for Children* provides an excellent listing of stories, categorized by country of origin.) Few of the folktales follow a predictable pattern, but they can certainly be shared with young children in read-aloud sessions. Teachers and students may also choose to work together to adapt some stories as Big Books useful for a variety of follow-up activities. Doing so will not only involve children in the culture depicted in each story but will also teach them a good deal about story structure.

Teachers should search for and use stories from a broad range of cultures, but it is particularly important to introduce books that reflect the backgrounds of the children in the class. Bishop

Stories from Around the World

- The books listed below, traditional folk stories as well as modern tales, are excellent choices for introducing a variety of cultures through shared book experiences.
- Verna Aardema's *Bringing the Rain to Kapiti Plain* and *Why Mosquitoes Buzz in People's Ears: A West African Tale* (both West African)
- José Aruego and Ariane Dewey's *Rockabye Crocodile* (Philippine)
- Betty Baker's *Rat Is Dead and Ant Is Sad* (Native American)
- Betsy Bang's *The Old Woman and the Red Pumpkin* (Indian)
- Bernice Chardiet's *Juan Bobo and the Pig* (Puerto Rican)
- Tomie dePaola's *Fin M'Coul, the Giant of Knockmany Hill* (Irish) and *The Prince of the Dolomites* (Italian)
- Paul Galdone's *The Monkey & the Crocodile: A Jakata Tale from India* (Indian)
- Mirra Ginsburg's *Mushrooms in the Rain* (Russian)
- Nonny Hogrogian's *One Fine Day* (Armenian)
- Ruth Hürllmann's *The Proud White Cat* (German)
- Arlene Mosel's *Tikki Tikki Tembo* (Chinese)
- Alexei Tolstoy's *The Great Big Enormous Turnip* (Russian)
- Taro Yashima's *Umbrella* (Japanese)
- Margot Zemach's *It Could Always Be Worse* (Yiddish)

(1987) explains, "Children who find their own life experiences mirrored in books receive an affirmation of themselves and their culture" (p. 61).

Day-to-Day Life

Regardless of their cultural backgrounds, people the world over share the need for adequate shelter. Library shelves are teeming with many excellent nonfiction resources on topics related to different peoples, their needs, and the ways they live. Teachers can take samples of these into the classroom for children to browse through. Mary Ann Hoberman's *A House Is a House for Me* and Joanna Cole's *This Is the Place for Me* are two predictable books that can be used for activities related to housing needs. Pairs of children might work cooperatively to create shape books related to this topic, for example.

Modes of transport is another popular topic for study in the early childhood social studies curriculum. Children are fascinated by the many different kinds of conveyances people use to go places and carry things. John Burningham's delightful *Mr. Gumpy's Outing* and *Mr. Gumpy's Motor Car* illustrate different types of transportation. A natural extension to reading these aloud would be for the children to create a Mr. Gumpy Big Book of their own—maybe entitled *Mr. Gumpy's Balloon Ride* or *Mr. Gumpy Goes Flying*.

First the teacher can ask the children what they know about hot-air balloons. Their knowledge may be surprisingly extensive. Encyclopedias and other reference materials can be checked for additional information. Burningham's two books have 12 characters each. Children may want to personalize their Big Book by "joining" Mr. Gumpy in their story. In any event, the children should decide on the characters and the adventure. If the teacher makes a tape recording of the children's story it will be easy later to print the text on large sheets of paper ready for illustrating. After the children have illustrated the pages and cover, the book can be fastened together and placed in the listening center, along with the tape recording.

Reading for Many Purposes

As stated previously, one of the great strengths of the shared book experience is its flexibility. High-quality children's books are available on virtually any topic; this means that teachers can use literature in both literacy instruction and in other subject areas. The tremendous increase in the number and variety of children's books published over the past decade gives teachers a broad range of outstanding resources to use for instruction across the curriculum.

The flexibility of the shared book experience also means that teachers can tailor follow-up activities to suit both the needs of students and those of the curriculum. A storybook read aloud may lead to activities related to studies in math, science, art, music, social studies, or any of the other subjects frequently taught at the early childhood level, all the while reinforcing instruction in reading and writing. Teachers are limited only by the books available to them, the needs and interests of their students, and their own imaginations.

The use of literature in all areas of the curriculum is important in another way. Outstanding children's trade books are an effective motivator; when children are exposed to good stories with fine illustrations, they are eager both to learn how to read the books themselves and to explore the subject matter the books describe. In addition, this approach teaches children that literacy abilities have concrete applications, and that being able to read means being able to find out about many different topics. Indeed, sharing books across the curriculum can lead to increased learning in all areas of early childhood education and will put young children on the road to reading for information and for pleasure.

CHAPTER SIX

Read-In Time

In discussing classroom writing, Calkins (1986) stresses the importance of reserving specific blocks of time for the activity and of adhering to an established overall routine. The teacher need not choreograph every step, but structuring the writing workshop and holding it regularly will lead to children learning what to expect; they will begin to anticipate the workshop and will come to school prepared to write.

In a similar way, a framework for organizing and managing the activities associated with the shared book experience can offer consistency and predictability to children as they develop into readers. In this chapter I describe such a framework—a managerial structure I call "read-in time"—and outline two theme units designed around it.

A Framework for Reading

Read-in time has four segments. It begins with an *orientation*, a time for the teacher to engage the mental energies of the children and channel their attention toward reading. During *reading time*, the children read alone or with a partner. In this second segment of the read-in, the teacher circulates among the children to offer help and then holds a few individual conferences. *Animating language* time encompasses a variety of activities in which the teacher encourages the children to become actively involved in learning and in using language in all its forms. During the final segment, *sharing*, all the children gather together to learn what different groups have been doing and listen to individuals share something they have found interesting.

These four segments are described in detail in the next sections of this chapter and are illustrated in the theme units presented later.

Orientation

During the orientation the teacher's job is to gain the children's interest—perhaps by inspiring them with a shared book experience—and to establish the tone for the literacy activities that will follow. The most common orientation activity is reading aloud from a Big Book, but teachers can also try any of the "getting started" activities described earlier in this volume. Story prediction, text and illustration comparison, echo reading, oral cloze procedures, or minilessons focusing on particular aspects of print revealed in a story are all appropriate for beginning the read-in time. Teachers may also want to use this time to announce different students' reading achievements. No matter what procedure is used, the orientation should be a time for lively discussion, snippets of wisdom and advice, and guidance for the later activities. (Note that while reading aloud is often the main orientation activity, it should not be confined exclusively to this segment of the read-in time. Teachers should also read to the children in their classes at other times throughout the day. Often teachers select short, predictable books for orientation and read longer, more complex books at other times.)

As with other reading activities, the orientation step should suit the needs and interests of each class. Conferences with individual children are a good place to pick up ideas for orientation activities. Teachers will need to experiment to find the format that works best for them; for instance, some teachers have found that lessons focusing on one idea or purpose are most effective for setting a tone for later reading.

Regardless of the activity, the orientation period usually lasts between five and ten minutes, although in special circumstances more time may be required. Teachers will know that the orientation has been successful if the children cannot wait to begin reading on their own.

Reading Time

Many educators have pointed out the importance of giving children ample time to read (see, for example, Allington, 1977; Anderson et al., 1985; Huck & Kerstetter, 1987; Slaughter, 1988; Trelease, 1989). Cullinan (1987) reasons, "The old saying 'Practice makes perfect' applies to reading as much as it does to anything else. Learning to read is like learning to play the piano: The more we practice, the better we become" (p. 12). Teale and Martinez (1988) observed that the emergent reading behaviors of kindergarten children increased significantly on those days when particular activities—such as reading to a partner or preparing to read a book to the teacher—were scheduled.

Unlike the orientation, reading time follows the same procedure for each read-in: the children read quietly, alone or with their partners, while the teacher holds a few individual conferences. During reading time, children should each have two or three books at their desks to read or look at. Every classroom should have its own library with a variety of reading materials from which the children can choose. Not all the choices have to be commercial trade books; teachers should include the children's own creations and such things as magazines or "anthologies" of selections cut from worn-out basal readers and bound together with attractive homemade covers. The permanent collection can be supplemented with a rotating supply of books borrowed from the school or community library. All the books should be displayed attractively in an easily visible and easy-to-reach spot.

Many teachers encourage children to select or exchange books when they first come into the classroom, before the read-in time orientation. Children may also be encouraged to bring in books from home or to take time during independent activities to select books for later read-ins. They should not select or exchange books during reading time, as this is a quiet time set aside just for reading. Teachers should probably keep a few extra books at their desks, however, for children who finish reading the materials they have selected on their own.

During this segment of the read-in, children will be working independently or in pairs. Teachers often find that a child will benefit from having a reading partner. Partners can provide important feedback and increase one another's interest in reading. In all likelihood, one of the partners will be a more competent reader and can serve as a private tutor for the less advanced child. For the more advanced child, teaching provides one of the best ways of solidifying newly acquired knowledge.

The teacher may want students to spend most of the reading time working independently, sharing with partners for only the last five minutes or so. Some teachers let a limited number of partners go off to different areas of the room to work quietly; others designate one day of the week as "partner day." Each teacher should use whatever procedure he or she finds most effective and least disruptive to reading time.

While children are busy reading, the teacher holds individual conferences. Teachers can often manage to see four to six students during reading time. If teachers keep a "conference schedule" on the chalkboard and at the beginning of the day read aloud the names of the children who will be called for conferences later on, the children will know what to expect. Some blank lines can be left on the schedule so children can request a conference if they have a special need or something to share.

For each conference, one child is called to the "conference table" (the teacher's desk or a table slightly removed from the children's desks). The child brings along one or more books, as well as any personal reading record he or she has been keeping. The teacher's task is to give the child positive feedback, regardless of his or her level of development. The conference provides an opportunity to offer encouragement and personal attention. This gives children the important message that the teacher is interested enough in what they are reading (or looking at) to give them special time and undivided attention. Children conclude that reading must be pretty important and strive to come to the conference with something positive to share. In addition, when the teacher interacts with a child, he or she models ways in which the child might interact with others. This modeling affects the ways children relate to their partners and other classmates. As these social interactions become easier, children will come to rely more on each other (at least for small matters) and less on the teacher. With time, they will begin to make more decisions for themselves and to take more responsibility for their own learning (Hansen, 1987).

To create this reassuring atmosphere in each conference, the teacher begins by encouraging the child to talk about books and reading. Typical questions include these:

- At the last conference you were reading _____ [looking at notes from a previous conference]. What are you reading now?
- Why did you select this particular book?
- Is it good?
- What's your book about?
- Would you read some of your book to me, please?
- What do you think will happen next?
- What book would you like to read next?
- How is your reading going?
- Is there anything I can do to help you with your reading?

At this point the teacher may suggest a book or two the child might enjoy, or may even have a book selected to offer the child. The teacher can also give the child a short lesson, although this should be very focused. Calkins and Harwayne (1987) offered this advice about writing conferences, which applies equally well to reading conferences: "Don't solve the problems of the world in a conference. Instead, treat a conference as a time to share one strategy, to give one tip, or to learn one thing about the [child]" (p. 60).

During each conference, the teacher should take brief notes. (A loose-leaf binder works well for this because pages can be added as required.) Gunderson (1990) recommends that teachers create "conference logs" to assist them in taking careful and accurate notes. The log provides space for the teacher to comment on the child's recall and comprehension of text, as well as for analysis of oral reading abilities and notation of skills that need improvement.

The entries included in each child's log might note the conference date, the titles of any books the child brought, thoughts on the child's oral reading or sharing, accomplishments or problems detected during the conference, recommendations for other books, and any instruction given. On a separate sheet of paper, the teacher can jot down ideas for brief lessons for future orientation periods. If one child seems ready for a lesson on a particular aspect of language, other children in the class would probably profit from the lesson also.

Children interpret this note-taking as an indication of the seriousness of the conference and of the teacher's interest in their progress. To supplement these notes, children—especially older ones—can keep records of their own reading: books they have read, their judgments about the books, and topics in which they are developing interests. The teacher's and the children's records together are enormously helpful in developing a comprehensive understanding of each child's interests and progress.

In addition to helping individuals, conferences have great value for the class as a whole. In these one-on-one situations, teachers are able to develop a more personal relationship with each child than would be possible in a classroom that arranged the children in ability groups and followed the regimented procedures suggested in many basal reading programs. These personal relationships produce an atmosphere of mutual trust that benefits everyone in the classroom.

Most teachers find that these one-on-one meetings let them accomplish a great deal in a short time. The length varies, but five minutes is usually enough for most conferences. A conference is successful if the child leaves the session feeling good about himself or herself and eager to read more books. If any time remains in this segment of the read-in, teachers can circulate around the room expressing interest in children's choices of books and their progress in reading them.

Reading time as a whole can last as long as the children are usefully occupied with their reading, with the duration increasing as the children become more mature and more interested in books. (Twenty-five minutes is probably about the maximum for children in the early primary grades.) When the teacher is aware that the children are becoming restless, it is time to move on to other activities.

Animating Language

The read-in's quiet reading time is followed by all sorts of lively classroom activities having to do with language learning. This "animating language" phase should last for about an hour. A broad range of whole-class, small-group, and independent activities—including such things as writing independently, creating artwork, "publishing" Big Books, working on pocket chart or scroll stories, and using reference books to find information on particular topics—

are appropriate for this portion of the read-in.

Whole-class activities will probably be limited to a teacher's presentation of new learning material or a "special event" (a cooking lesson, for example) that requires considerable supervision. Dividing the class into smaller groups to work on specific projects has three advantages. First, many of the animating language activities appropriate for the shared book experience work best when about eight children participate. Second, when children complete activities in collaboration with their peers and without the direct involvement of the teacher, they develop social skills, self-reliance, and self-discipline. Third, the rest of the class serves as a natural audience for each group's presentation of completed activities, providing a real reason for creating. The animating language portion of the read-in time also lends itself to a variety of activities children can undertake on their own or in pairs.

When children are working alone or in small groups, it can be helpful to structure activities around classroom learning centers. These are specially designated areas containing materials and tools needed for children to pursue particular tasks. The library is the learning center most commonly found in early childhood classrooms, but there are many other possibilities.

The *listening center*, for example, is an area where small groups of children gather to listen to tape recordings made to accompany Big Books and other predictable literature. To avoid disrupting other activities, this center should be somewhat removed from the heart of the class or should contain a few sets of headphones. The center can also have a filmstrip projector and a phonograph to accommodate commercially produced record-book and record-filmstrip combinations. With a little guidance, even children as young as kindergarten-age can be taught to use these pieces of equipment responsibly. It is helpful to have storage facilities at this center to hold tapes and records, as well as the books and filmstrips that go along with them.

A less common area in the classroom is the *recording center*, used for children, alone or with a partner, to read a story onto a tape. This provides incentive for children to practice their oral reading and may give the hesitant child more confidence in his or her ability. Ideally, each child should have his or her own tape for this activity.

The *writing center* should be an integral part of every early childhood classroom (Teale & Sulzby, 1989). This area is equipped with everything a child needs to write: pencils, crayons, felt-tipped pens, chalk and chalkboard, a typewriter or computer (if possible), scissors, stapler, paper brads, yarn and a hole-punch (for binding pages together to make books), metal rings, magazines, newspapers, and lots of paper. Martinez and Teale (1987) recommend that kindergarten children be given only unlined paper at the beginning of the school year because it delivers no signals about how it should be used. Calkins (1986) notes, "Teachers...find that, because writing materials significantly influence what and how children write, simply changing the shape and size of available paper can pose new challenges for children" (p. 27). Later on, teachers can introduce different types of paper, such as long strips; blank mini-books; booklets made from graph paper, paper bags, or dark construction paper; stationery and envelopes; strips of colored paper taped together into scrolls; booklets in the shape of diamonds, triangles, circles, and octagons; sheets of unlined paper, lined paper, story paper (half blank, half lined), or construction paper; and sheets from wallpaper sample books.

Children also find it helpful to have an adjustable date stamp and a stamp pad in the writing center so they can easily date their work. For younger children, the center can also contain magnetic or wooden letters; for older children, book-binding supplies (and instructions for their use) should be available. If the writing center is located near the art center, children can work on drawing and writing together more easily, using some of the same materials for both.

The *art center* is vital to many activities associated with read-in time and the shared book experience. Children will be creating books, and they should have everything they need to make the illustrations. As with the writing center, teachers can bring out certain materials during specific times and encourage children to try different techniques.

A *drama and dress-up area* is very popular with younger children. This can house a puppet theater and a variety of puppets (both commercial and child-made), boxes of old clothes and hats, lengths of fabric, and an assortment of props. From time to time, this center can become theme-oriented; for a summer holiday theme, for example, it could feature travel posters, magazines, and brochures, as well as appropriate items of clothing (Teale & Sulzby, 1989). Writing materials should also be made available to children in the drama area (Vukelich, 1990)—and, for that matter, in other centers.

Independent activities designed to go with predictable books can be kept in the *independent task center*. If classroom space is limited, a child can take one of these activities and its accompanying book to the area used for orientation and sharing. *Mathematics, science*, and *social studies centers* can also be informal, perhaps consisting only of one or more tables for display and exploration. These areas can be changed periodically to reflect the themes or units under study.

Providing space for all these learning centers is clearly no easy task. While no one arrangement will suit all teachers, the floor plan shown in Figure 6 presents an idea of how a room can be set up to accommodate a range of animating language activities. The desks are pushed to one part of the room to make as much space as possible for the learning centers. Double-sided bookshelves (on wheels), about waist high, make ideal dividers between the centers while providing extra space for storage and display.

Because of the wide range of activities possible in this portion of the read-in time, teachers and students alike will need to find some way to manage their time. It is useful to provide children with some guidance on the sorts of activities appropriate for each animating

Figure 6
A Sample Floor Plan

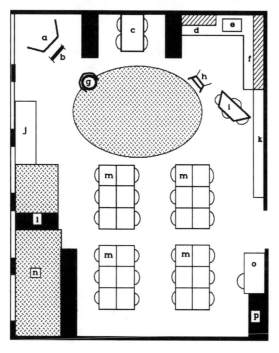

Key

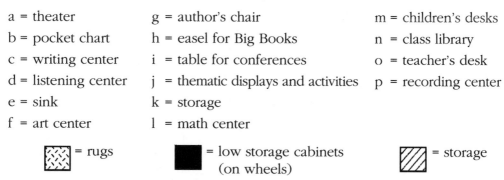

a = theater	g = author's chair	m = children's desks
b = pocket chart	h = easel for Big Books	n = class library
c = writing center	i = table for conferences	o = teacher's desk
d = listening center	j = thematic displays and activities	p = recording center
e = sink	k = storage	
f = art center	l = math center	

▨ = rugs   ■ = low storage cabinets (on wheels)   ▨ = storage

session; these activities can be linked to the book or books highlighted in the orientation, and their number can increase as children become more mature and independent. Teachers often prepare a "Things to Do" chart listing the available activities and update this when necessary.

Teachers will also need to devise a way to keep track of which activities each child has undertaken. One teacher rescued an easel that was being discarded, gave it a quick spray painting, and put it to use as both a Things to Do chart and a way of monitoring the children's activities. On the easel she mounted a board with the learning centers listed in a column on the left. Beside the centers she attached long pockets made from strips of cardboard, writing a numeral on each to indicate the number of children who could work in that center at any one time. During the first animating language session, she gave each child a card with his or her name written on it and told the students to place their cards in the pocket for the center they would be working in. (The pockets were long and shallow enough that the names showed above them.)

Now each morning when the children enter the classroom, they remove their name cards from the chart and take them to their seats. (The names that remain provide the teacher with a list of children who are absent.) The teacher then asks the children to choose the centers in which they would like to work during that day's animating language period. If a special activity is available at one of the centers, the teacher asks who has not yet had an opportunity to work there and has those children place their name cards first. The teacher reports an additional advantage to the approach: when language activities are finished and some centers have not been tidied up, it is easy to check on who worked in those areas.

Other teachers devise "contracts" in which children agree to undertake a certain number of listed activities. These contracts have the advantage of being specific and easily changed with the theme or types of activities planned for the week. Asking children to indicate in writing that they have completed an activity can sometimes spur them to be very responsible about their work.

Checklists are also a popular way to provide structure for animating language activities. Names of students can be listed across the top of the chart and the activities down the left. Children then can simply check off the activities they have completed.

Finally, when numerous activities are going on simultaneously in the classroom, teachers can find the atmosphere a bit chaotic. Specific rules of behavior should therefore be established and explained. Hunter-Grundin (1989) recommends telling children that "the most important rule, which applies to all center work, is that no one in the classroom should be able to hear you except for the people you are working with" (p. 28). Often the teacher needs only to remind a child that he or she is being too noisy and is bothering others for order to be restored. If the noise increases or if the talk in a particular group does not appear to be task-related, the teacher can join the children to help them reestablish direction (Goodman, 1986). The children may have a problem that is preventing them from continuing, or they may simply need an adult presence to get them back on track. Many teachers find that when children have a choice of centers in which to work and are free to move to a different area when one project is complete, they are much more inclined to conform to the rules and to persevere with their tasks.

Sharing

In this five- to ten-minute portion of the read-in time, selected children or small groups present the projects they have been working on to the rest of the class. This may involve such things as reading aloud a story or story-in-progress, sharing an interesting fact learned from a book, putting on a play, or describing how a creation made in the art center relates to a favorite story. Just as children in a writing workshop share their stories, so should emerging and developing readers be given opportunities to share their achievements and discoveries.

This important sharing time is similar to show-and-tell. It allows presenting children to express themselves and enhance their speaking skills, while audience members have the opportunity to develop listening and oral comprehension skills. Sharing is also a great motivator: an appreciative audience provides a wonderful incentive for children to do their best in language activities.

Evaluating Progress

Any evaluation procedure should provide teachers with information about the things their students are learning and an idea of how successful their teaching has been. To assess a child's growth in writing, the teacher can collect samples of work over the course of the year, but no such collection of work is possible with reading. Teachers can, however, gather observations, anecdotal records, and lists of accomplishments to yield insights about each child's progress. More specifically, teachers can keep files for each child containing notes taken during individual confer-

ences, writing samples produced during animating language activities, records of oral readings (including information on miscues), notes about (or tapes of) story retellings, anecdotal observations, and notes about the child's performance on such activities as cloze exercises (Holdaway, 1984).

Children's development is invariably uneven. Sometimes weeks will pass during which a child will seem to be hardly progressing at all. Then for some reason the child will surge ahead and make enormous gains, as if everything has suddenly fallen into place. Meanwhile, another child who has been progressing at a steady pace may all at once find himself or herself struggling and slipping. Perhaps the child has decided to try more difficult reading materials, perhaps there are problems external to school, or perhaps this is just part of normal progression for this child. Notes kept over time help teachers put these surges and slumps into perspective and should provide practical information on ways to help each child.

Asking a series of questions periodically is also useful for evaluating a child's progress. The following questions are appropriate when the read-in time procedure is being used:

- Does the child enjoy reading? Is the child eager to read with his or her partner?
- Does the child appear to read at home? Does he/she select to work in the classroom library as an optional activity?
- Is the child willing and anxious to share information from books?

103

- Does he/she volunteer to read aloud to the class?
- Does the child usually select books that are within his/her reading capabilities?
- Is the child able to retell a story in his/her own words?
- What kinds of strategies does the child use to figure out unknown words?
- Does he/she actively participate in different language activities?
- Is he/she able to complete tasks independently?

Lamme (1987) suggests that teachers ask themselves these further questions when evaluating emergent readers:

- Does the child show an interest in words? Is he/she able to point to individual words on a page? Is he/she able to turn the pages at the appropriate time when the story is being played on a tape recorder?
- Can the child locate familiar books?
- Is the child able to read common words? Does the child ask questions about print? Does he or she seem to be aware that print has meaning?

Teachers can prepare a list of questions for each child in the class. Then at regular intervals throughout the year, they go through the lists and indicate responses; these lists become part of each child's file. To record achievements in writing, Calkins (1986) recommends that

teachers create "can do" lists (Audrey can: write her name; begin each sentence with a capital letter; and so on); similar lists can be created to track a child's progress in reading.

Holdaway (1984) argues that this type of observation-based assessment is both more precise and more fair than absolute reliance on scores from standardized tests. In addition, these procedures do not dampen children's enthusiasm the way test scores sometimes can. To make the most of this advantage, comparisons and rankings of the different children in the class should be avoided. A child's development in literacy should be measured as parents judge their children's early growth and achievements: by finding out what that child can do today that he or she could not do before.

Theme Units

Many early childhood teachers build some of their instruction around theme units, using one topic to focus children's learning across the curriculum. These units are of a fixed length and occupy much classroom time for their duration. As described earlier in this volume, the flexibility of the shared book experience means that it can be integrated across disciplines; it is therefore an effective overall approach to use when designing theme units. In addition, the read-in time procedure can provide structure for implementing these units as well as a means of monitoring children's progress.

In the remainder of this chapter I provide two examples of theme units, one structured around a particular book and the second focusing on a single topic. The description of these units is intended to provide teachers with ideas for developing their own units. As with all instruction at the early childhood level, theme units should be designed to accommodate the needs and interests of particular students and teachers while providing instruction appropriate to the overall curriculum.

Rosie's Walk across the Curriculum

It was the third week of school. At this point in the year, one of Edna Thomas's primary objectives was to persuade her first graders to work more independently. She wanted to encourage the children to take some responsibility for their own learning and to become more self-reliant; she also wanted to "personalize" instruction and give more time to individuals and small groups. Thomas decided that a week-long theme unit organized around read-in time would provide an ideal way of fulfilling her objectives. Because her students seemed ready to explore notions of authorship, Thomas decided to focus the theme unit on the works of one author—Pat Hutchins—and specifically on the book *Rosie's Walk*. With this unit, she intended to offer the children many opportunities to grow in all facets of language and, through collaborative activities and special projects, to further learning in many curricular areas. Thomas made a chart (shown in Figure 7 on the next page) outlining the highlights of the theme unit; this helped her visualize classroom organization and how the read-in time would be managed, especially the work the children would be doing in the animating language sessions.

Implementing the theme unit required a fair amount of advance preparation. Thomas first purchased one enlarged copy and six smaller copies of *Rosie's Walk*; she also borrowed several other books by Pat Hutchins from her colleagues and from her own collection of children's literature. (Hutchins's books include *Don't Forget the Bacon!*, *The Doorbell Rang*, *Good-Night, Owl!*, *The Surprise Party*, and *What Game Shall We Play?*, all of which are popular among emergent and developing readers.) Next Thomas obtained 23 different books on farms and farm animals—both fiction and nonfiction—from the school and local libraries. To all of the books she affixed removable red circle stickers, so they could be easily distinguished from the other books in the class library; then she set up a special table to display the collection. Finally Thomas prepared two games ("spell it out" and "make a match"), two "Things to Do" check-off charts, tape recordings of *Rosie's Walk* and *The Surprise Party*, a stencil of a hen for creating shape books, six labels for the "follow the sign" activity, short poems about animals written on chart paper, and various supplies for art projects.

Thomas followed the same basic plan of operation throughout the week. Each day's orientation helped the children tune in to the read-in time procedure. This was followed by a period designated for quiet reading during which children read alone or with their partners, or met with Thomas for individual conferences. A variety of whole-class and small-group activities relating to reading and language came next, and a

Figure 7
Managing the Read-In Time

Monday	Tuesday	Wednesday	Thursday	Friday

Orientation (about 10 minutes)

Monday	Tuesday	Wednesday	Thursday	Friday
Read *Rosie's Walk* Big Book; echo reading	Reread *Rosie's Walk* Big Book; focus on the letters *R* and *H*	Read two other books by Hutchins; pass out Hutchins books and focus on illustrations	Reread *Rosie's Walk* using oral cloze; animal classification game	Follow-the-sign game; share poems

Reading Time (15 to 25 minutes)
Children to read quietly by themselves or with a partner. Hold individual
conferences with children.

Animating Language (about an hour)

Monday	Tuesday	Wednesday	Thursday	Friday
Whole class: writing workshop Independent: listening center, class library, red circle books, spell-it-out game	Group A*: *Rosie's Walk* mural Group B: writing Group C: select from Things to Do chart (Groups B and C to switch halfway through)	Group A: mural Group B*: *The Surprise Party* puppet show Group C: select from Things to Do chart	Group A: select from Things to Do chart Group B: puppets Group C*: *Henry's Walk* Big Book	Whole class: no-bake cookies; language experience exercise

Sharing (5 to 10 minutes)

Monday	Tuesday	Wednesday	Thursday	Friday
Volunteers share drafts of Rosie shape stories or interesting books they have encountered	Group A tells about mural; volunteers share Rosie shape stories or interesting books	Group A shares mural; volunteers share Rosie shape stories or interesting books	Group B presents puppet show	Group C presents *Henry's Walk* Big Book; all children share cookies

* indicates the group receiving most of the teacher's attention; other children are working independently

sharing session concluded every read-in time. Once Thomas had gathered the materials and had decided how this special week would be managed, it was time to begin the theme unit.

Monday

Thomas began the first day's orientation by reading the Big Book version of *Rosie's Walk* to the children. In the story, Rosie the hen strolls through the farmyard, unaware that she is being followed by a hungry fox. The threat of the fox is conveyed almost entirely through the illustrations, and so as Thomas read the words, she encouraged the children to react to the pictures. The children found much to talk about in these pictures, so complex are they in comparison to the text. Thomas then reread the story and invited the children to join in through a variation of the echo reading procedure: first she read a whole page, then she asked the children to repeat the words as she pointed to each one.

Now came reading time. On this first day, Thomas asked the children to take from their desks any books they would like to read. She also distributed the six smaller copies of *Rosie's Walk* to different children, as well as the special "red circle" books she had gathered. She made sure that each child had three to five books. While the children read quietly, Thomas had the opportunity to meet with four children individually.

The reading time lasted as long as the children read quietly, about fifteen minutes—not too bad for the first weeks of first grade. When the children seemed to be getting restless, Thomas finished the fourth individual conference, collect-ed all the special books, and asked the children to put their own books away.

Now Thomas asked for the whole class's attention so she could explain what would happen next. First she displayed the "Things to Do" check-off chart. This record-keeping device is designed to show children what activities are available and to help them account for the ones they have completed. Over the years, Thomas has found that this technique helps children become more responsible for completing independent activities. In addition, being able to check off things they have done gives children a sense of accomplishment.

Thomas had already prepared two of these charts, one for the boys and one for the girls. She had learned in previous years that one chart listing *all* the names was too difficult for the children to use; dividing the chart into two made it easier for each child to locate his or her name. Thomas also knew from experience that it was best to save some activities for later in the week rather than listing them all at the outset; this prevented children from being overwhelmed with choices while they were still becoming familiar with both the read-in time and the idea of a theme unit.

Now Thomas explained that the whole class was going to engage in a writing workshop and that if some students finished writing before the rest of the class, they could occupy themselves quietly with one of the independent activities listed on the chart. These she read aloud. On this Monday, the Things to Do chart looked like that in Figure 8 on the next page. (Note that the boys' and girls' charts listed the same activities.)

Figure 8
Monday's Things to Do Check-off Chart

You may do these things (remember to put a check under your name when you finish something)	Greg	Tommy	Mario	Tat-Ying	Enrico	LeVar	Hank	Samuel	Tony
pick a book to read from our library									
pick a red circle book to read									
listen to the tape of _Rosie's Walk_									
play the Spell-it-out game									

Thomas then quickly reminded the children where materials for the various activities could be found and explained how the spell-it-out (key word) game was played. Finally, she told the children that she would help them keep track of their activities on the check-off chart at first but that later in the week they would be responsible for doing this themselves.

Now it was time for the writing workshop. Thomas showed the children the hen stencil and paper they could use to make Rosie shape books and demonstrated how to put such a book together. As a prewriting activity to stimulate the children's ideas, Thomas asked the children these questions:

- What would you like to write about in a book shaped like this?
- What can you tell us about hens?
- What other animals live on farms?

She jotted down a few of their ideas and read them over with the children. She then asked the children to express their own ideas in pictures and words.

While the children worked to make their shape books and began writing, Thomas circulated among them. She managed to speak briefly with each child, commenting on progress, giving assistance as necessary, and helping the children clarify the ideas they were trying to express. When individual children felt they had finished their books or began to get restless, Thomas encouraged them to try something from the check-off chart. After about an hour the children all seemed to need a change, so Thomas moved on to sharing time.

All the children were called back to the classroom's central carpeted area. Thomas found that some of the children were anxious to sit in the author's chair to share the Rosie stories they had started and show the pictures they had created. Three other children wanted to share interesting books they had become involved in during reading time. Thomas gave all these children positive responses and encouraged the other children to do likewise. Finally she went to the check-off charts and asked if anyone had forgotten to indicate an activity he or she had completed. The day's read-in time had lasted nearly two hours;

Books on Farms and Farm Animals

Below are a few recommended books about farms and farm animals. Some of these were included in the collection of "red circle" books that Edna Thomas gathered for her theme unit.

- *The New Baby Calf* (Edith Newlin Chase and Barbara Reid)
- *Animals Everywhere* (Ingri D'Aulaire and Edgar P. D'Aulaire)
- *Hard Scrabble Harvest* (Dahlov Ipcar)
- *The Little Farm* (Lois Lenski)
- *A Single Speckled Egg* (Sonia Levitin)
- *A Treeful of Pigs* (Arnold Lobel)
- *My Day on the Farm* (Chiyoko Nakatani)
- *The Year at Maple Hill Farm* (Alice Provensen and Martin Provensen)
- *Animals on the Farm* (Feodor Rojankovsky)
- *More Potatoes!* (Millicent E. Selsam)
- *What's Inside of Animals?* (Herbert S. Zim)

now it was time to move on to an entirely different activity.

Tuesday

On the second day of the theme unit, Thomas started off by rereading the *Rosie's Walk* Big Book, with assistance from the children. She then wrote the letter *R* at the top of a piece of chart paper and the letter *H* on a second piece. She passed out the small copies of *Rosie's Walk* to six different children and asked them to look for words beginning with the target letters. They were able to find *Rosie, hen,* and *haystack.* Meanwhile Thomas asked the other children if any of their names began with R or H, which resulted in two more words being written on the chart paper. Then the children began to suggest other words beginning with these letters. When the children had come up with 11 words for each chart, Thomas helped them read over the entire list.

Now Thomas distributed the red circle books; six children who had not had a chance to see a copy of *Rosie's Walk* on Monday were given the smaller books at this time. As the children read alone or with their partners, Thomas held six individual reading conferences.

At the start of Tuesday's animating language period Thomas read over the selections on the Things to Do chart. Two new activities were listed: a recording station and the make-a-match game. Thomas showed the children how to play the new word game, encouraging them to make matches between the illustration and text cards and to find the corresponding words in the *Rosie's Walk* Big Book. Thomas also showed the children the tape recorder set up at the recording station. This was to be used only for reading and playing back stories on tape. The children were shown how to load their tapes and which buttons to push. A child who had a similar tape recorder at home offered to assist classmates if they had problems.

Thomas then divided the class into three groups of approximately equal size. Today she would work directly with Group A to help those children start a mural based on *Rosie's Walk*. The other two groups were to alternate their activities. For the first half of the animating language time, the children in Group B would work at their desks on their Rosie shape books. They were encouraged to bring any questions to their reading partners first, rather than coming directly to Thomas. Group C children were to select from the independent activities on the Things to Do chart. The two groups would then switch places and activities about halfway through the period.

After making sure that everyone knew what to work on, Thomas asked the Group A children to come to the back of the room where they would have space to create their mural. She had already cut a piece of brown packing paper to cover one of the room's bulletin boards, where the finished mural was to be mounted; she had also gathered sponges, paint, construction paper, scraps of giftwrap, wallpaper from sample books, scissors, glue, crayons, pencils, a stapler, chart paper, and felt pens.

Thomas started the activity with a planning stage, similar to the prewriting phase of the writing workshop. She asked the children to recall some of the characters and things they remembered from *Rosie's Walk* and listed their recollections on the chart paper. Next she asked the children how they wanted their mural to appear: should there be one Rosie and one Fox or several of each, depicting the different incidents in the book? They decided on the first option. Then Thomas had the children select the characters and features they wanted to create and wrote the appropriate name beside each item listed on the chart paper. This list was saved; the children would use it later to make labels for their mural.

Now it was time to think about the mural in more detail. Thomas explained how to make a background by sponging on thinned paint to create a unified effect. She advised the children to let one color (for the sky, for instance) dry before painting with another color (say, for the trees). Once again she encouraged the children to plan ahead. What did they want to put in the background? (They did not have to include any of the things listed on the chart, which would be cut from different kinds of paper and pasted on the mural later.) Where would the ground be? Would they put in trees? Would they paint a pond or cut one from colored paper? Would all of them be involved in the sponge painting or would some children paint the background and some work on the cut-out characters and objects?

During the remainder of the animating language time that day, the children completed the background painting. The painting went very quickly because the children used large sponges to dab on the paint, creating an interesting and attractive mottled effect. The children had also had time to begin working on the characters and other things listed on the chart they had made at the beginning of the session. Thomas cautioned the children against making the cut-outs too small: Rosie, for example, had to be at least 12 inches (30 cm) tall to be seen clearly from the other side of the room.

While the children in Group A were busy working on their own, Thomas went to see how Groups B and C were progressing. She had some time to interact with a few of the children who were working on shape books and checked to see whether any children had completed independent learning activities.

For sharing time on this day, Thomas asked children from Group A to tell the rest of the class what they had been doing. In addition, some of the children in Groups B and C wanted to share the Rosie shape stories they had written. Two children were encouraged to share books they had found interesting, and one child played a tape she had made of *Rosie's Walk.*

Thomas asked the children in Groups B and C whether the centers were working well or whether there were problems in any of them. (She always asks for feedback about the centers because this helps her create better and more independent activities for the children.) Finally, since several children had completed activities, Thomas helped them place marks in the correct spaces on the check-off chart.

Wednesday

From her collection of books by Pat Hutchins, Thomas selected *Don't Forget* the Bacon! and Good-Night, Owl! to read aloud for Wednesday's orientation. She then passed out these two books, the six copies of Rosie's Walk, and copies of other books by Hutchins. When Thomas asked the children to focus on the pictures, they were able to detect many similarities in illustrations from different books. Thomas also read aloud some information from the book jackets about the artist/author and showed the class a photograph of Hutchins. The children were very curious; for many of them this was the first time they fully understood that a real person had created all these books. Then Thomas asked the children to read quietly for a while. As they did so, Thomas held seven individual conferences.

After about 20 minutes the children were ready for something more active. The children in Group A had work to finish on their Rosie's Walk mural. All the equipment was out and ready for the children to finish the cut-out characters and objects, arrange them on the background, and paste them in place. The children were also to label all the cut-outs by copying the words from the chart onto strips of paper and pasting these near the appropriate items on the mural. (They could also identify other objects they had included.) Thomas asked them if they thought they would have any problems if they worked on their own and addressed the concerns they raised. Before moving on, she told them that they could return to their seats to work on their Rosie shape books when they had completed the mural.

The children in Group C were asked to select from among the independent activities on the Things to Do chart or to continue work on their shape books.

Thomas would be working closely with the children in Group B today. She asked them to come with her to the back of the classroom, where she read aloud Hutchins's The Surprise Party. Then she asked the children if they would like to put on a surprise puppet-show version of the story for the class. They responded enthusiastically. Thomas had decided that stick puppets would be easiest for the children to create and had collected the equipment and materials they would need. She had also fashioned a puppet theater from a cardboard box lid (it was about six inches deep) by simply cutting out a large window in it (to serve as the "stage") and decorating the front. The lid was then placed on its end on a desk and taped down, so the children would be concealed behind it when they presented their show.

Each of the children in the group selected a character to create and act. The Surprise Party has seven characters; because Group B had eight members, Thomas thought it might be a good idea to have "twin squirrels." Two children volunteered to create squirrel puppets and to say their dialogue (more or less) together.

To create their puppets, the children were to cut out outlines of their characters and decorate them. Thomas had collected old file folders to use for the characters, as well as construction paper, wallpaper, giftwrap, yarn, crayons, felt pens, and glue for decorating. She advised each child to make his or her character large enough to be seen clearly from a distance, and then let the children go to work on their own.

112

The finished characters were to be stapled onto rulers to create stick puppets. For the actual performance, Thomas would serve as the moderator and read the major portion of the text while each child recited or ad libbed dialogue for his or her character and moved a puppet around the stage. The children received copies of the text, with their words highlighted, from which to practice. To increase their familiarity with the story, the children listened to a tape recording of it while they worked on their puppets.

As soon as Group B was working independently, Thomas went to see how the children in Group A were progressing with their mural. She helped them fix the last of the labels into place and then mounted the mural on the bulletin board. Next she checked on the children who were involved with independent activities and spoke with some of them about their writing projects (primarily the Rosie shape stories).

Thomas then returned to the puppet makers and asked them to rehearse the dialogue with her. She read *The Surprise Party* again, pausing periodically for the children to fill in some of the words. She did not expect the children to recite the exact text—a very entertaining performance would be possible even if they were able to remember only the gist of their lines.

When Thomas noticed that some of the children were becoming restless, she called the class together for sharing time. She announced that Group B was working on a surprise project and would have it ready for everyone on Thursday. The children in Group A were ready to share their mural with the class. First Thomas asked different children to read the labels they had attached to their mural; then she asked them to describe how they had created the background and the cut-out characters. Three children wanted to share their Rosie shape stories, and five others wanted to read a book or share a picture they had found interesting. Thomas then reminded children who had completed independent activities to mark them off on the check-off chart.

Thursday

For Thursday's orientation, Thomas reread *Rosie's Walk*, pausing at certain words and waiting for the children to fill them in. Then she went through the book again and asked for volunteers to read different pages while she pointed to the words.

Thomas next took out materials she had made for a pocket chart classification game. She had printed "Farm Animals" and "Wild Animals" on two cards, which she put in the top pocket of the chart. She asked the children to name different animals and wrote these names on blank cards. Then she asked the children to place the cards under either the wild animal or the farm animal heading.

For reading time, Thomas distributed the special books from the display table. She held six individual conferences as the children read alone or with their partners.

At the outset of the animating language session, Thomas again read the list of activities on the Things to Do chart. The pocket chart classification game had been added. The children in Group A selected from among the different independent activities; Group B children finished creating their puppets and then returned to their seats to work on their Rosie shape books.

The children in Group C were assembled to create a new Big Book based on *Rosie's Walk*. Thomas had selected the name Henry for the new main character because of its similarity to the word *hen*. The children decided that Henry was going to be a rabbit and that he would take a walk around a playground, stalked by a mean-looking dog. The group used the language experience approach to write the new story—the children expressed a series of ideas orally and Thomas wrote down their words. The result went something like this:

> Henry the rabbit went for a walk. Up the ladder. Down the slide. On the swing. Under the rings. Over the seesaw. Across the sandbox. And got back home in time for ice cream.

Because the words were few in number, Thomas was able to write each sentence or phrase directly on a sheet of enlarged paper. Once the children had finished dictating their story, Thomas helped them read over the whole text. Then the group talked about the kinds of illustrations that would be appropriate and each child took a page to illustrate. Early finishers worked on the front and back covers and title page. Finally, the names of all the children in Group C were listed as the authors and illustrators on the front cover and title page of *Henry's Walk*.

While this group was busy with its illustrations, Thomas checked on Group B's puppet making. She made sure the puppets were properly attached to the rulers and got the box-lid theater into place. Thomas read *The Surprise Party* again as the children filled in their lines and practiced with their puppets. This was the dress rehearsal.

As Group B made its last-minute preparations, Thomas checked on the children in Group A who were working on independent activities and observed the progress of Group C's *Henry's Walk*.

Thomas announced to the class that the children in Group B were ready to share their surprise. The rest of the children gathered around the puppet theater and Thomas showed them a copy of *The Surprise Party*. When the puppeteers were ready, Thomas began reading the story as rehearsed, with the different children holding up their puppets and saying their lines. The children found the puppet show highly entertaining, even if it wasn't a complete surprise. The show created even more of an impact because it was the only activity shared during this time.

Friday

To get the children tuned in on the last day of the theme unit, Thomas had devised a "follow the sign" game that let students march around the room on a specified route. She had designated different spots in the room as places or objects from *Rosie's Walk* and had labeled these appropriately: the "yard" was a piece of left-over mural paper taped to the floor; a piece of blue paper taped to a different part of the floor was labeled the "pond"; the "haystack" was a small table; the "mill" was Thomas's desk; a space between two children's desks was designated the "fence"; and the legs of another desk were "beehives." Thomas had also gathered six of the phrase strips from the make-a-match game; the phrases on these strips explained the directions Rosie took on her walk.

Before the activity began, Thomas passed out the phrase strips to six children. Then she split the remaining students into two groups and told them that they were to march along Rosie's route, following the instructions of the sign holders. Once the labels were in place and the first group of marchers was ready, Thomas called on each of the phrase-strip holders in turn to hold his or her sign high. The marchers did whatever the phrase strip said—for example, when a child held up "over the haystack," the children climbed one at a time on top of and over the designated table. The next phrase strip sent the marchers walking "around the pond." When the first group of marchers had followed all the phrase-strip directions, these children sat down and the other children had a chance to march around and follow the signs.

The children became quite lively during this activity. Afterwards, Thomas read them a few short poems about animals to calm them down and get them ready for reading time. She had printed copies of these poems on chart paper, and during a second reading, she pointed to the words and encouraged the children to join in for a choral reading. Then she read one poem again, two lines at a time, and asked the children to identify the rhyming words. These she underlined with colored markers.

The children were now relaxed and ready to read. Thomas distributed the red circle books and made sure that each child had a good supply of reading material. As they read alone or with partners, she held reading conferences with five more children. During the week Thomas had been able to confer with each child at least once.

Thomas thought that a change of pace would be a good idea and so had decided that the class would make cookies during today's animating language session. Since all of the children were going to participate, there was no need for a Things to Do chart. Instead, Thomas told the children that because it was Friday they would be doing something special to celebrate the end of "Rosie Week."

Thomas decided not to show the recipe for the no-bake refrigerator cookies to the children but to ask them to help make the cookies by following verbal directions. She would then have the children recall what they did—in effect creating a recipe through a language experience exercise. The children in the class were very much involved in the preparation of the dough, and all were able to help somehow. While the cookies were chilling, Thomas asked the children to imagine that they wanted to make these cookies at home and had to explain the procedure to their parents. What would they say? Thomas wrote down each statement in the order in which it was mentioned. This was how the first draft of the recipe appeared:

- Melt the marshmallows.
- Melt the butter and the sugar, too.
- Measure the cereal.
- Measure the nuts and mix them up.
- Put them in the refrigerator.
- Put the pan on the stove and stir it.

- Here is the recipe Thomas used for the no-bake refrigerator cookies. She chose this recipe because it has many steps in which the children can participate (these steps are indicated by asterisks within the recipe). Thomas brought a portable electric burner in from home for one of the steps and supervised the children carefully when they were near it. The cookies were chilled in the staffroom fridge.

    Measure* 5 cups of cereal flakes and 1 cup of chopped nuts and pour* into a large bowl. Stir.* Measure* 1 cup of margarine, 1 cup of white sugar, ½ cup of brown sugar, and 2 cups of marshmallow pieces and pour* into a heavy saucepan. Cook over low heat, stirring* constantly until the margarine and marshmallows melt and the sugar dissolves. Pour* this mixture over the cereal-nut mixture and stir* until well coated. Drop by spoonfuls* onto waxed paper and press* to flatten slightly. Refrigerate for about one hour before serving.

Since much vital information was missing and the directions were out of order (to put it mildly!), Thomas cut these statements apart and helped the children put them in the correct sequence. The children then needed to add to the directions and revise their statements to make the recipe coherent. She also helped the children to specify quantities. In the end, they taped together all the bits of chart paper and had a readable recipe. Thomas made copies of this recipe for the children.

Nearly an hour had passed, so the cookies were served while the boys and girls in Group C read *Henry's Walk* to the rest of the children. Then Thomas asked the Group C children to play "teacher" and try some of the activities she had used with the class. The children actually tried an oral cloze reading of *Henry's Walk!* Some of the children who had not had an opportunity to read their Rosie shape books did so at this time.

Evaluating Children and Teacher

During a theme unit like this, children are involved in all the components of language: listening, speaking, reading, and writing. In order to make informal assessments of the children's abilities in these areas, Thomas asked herself these questions:

- **Listening:** Was the child attentive during story time? How well did he or she listen to other children when they were sharing books or stories they had written?

- **Speaking:** Did the child seem to participate fully with partners or in small-group encounters? Was the child forthcoming in the individual conference? Did he or she make comments about any of the books? Did the child express him/herself during sharing time? Did he or she contribute to language experience exercises?

- **Reading:** Was it possible to detect areas of progress in reading during the conference? Were there areas of difficulty? Was the child eager to read/share his or her book? Did the child persist in reading during reading time? Did the child attempt to read *Rosie's Walk*? Was the child reading the words or attending only to the illustrations? Did the child read a story onto tape?

- **Writing:** Was any growth apparent in the child's writing of the Rosie shape story? Was the child able to express his or her thoughts so that they could be understood by others? Was the child receptive to ideas for revision? Was the child willing to persist through a second draft?

Thomas also noted the extent to which each child seemed to be working independently and observed the charts indicating the activities that had been completed by each.

Overall, Thomas was pleased with the children's progress over the week. They had clearly enjoyed and profited from many of the activities, and she was satisfied that she had moved toward her goal of encouraging self-reliance and independence in learning.

Into the Dragon's Lair

Although Edna Thomas's theme unit touched on many areas in the grade one curriculum, its primary focus was on literacy learning. Another teacher, Terry Calder, designed a theme unit that more explicitly encompassed different subjects.

Calder had been using the shared book experience with her combined grade one/two class since the beginning of the year. She had long been interested in the Middle Ages and in stories of knights, castles, and intrigue. She decided to create a unit around the theme of dragons because she thought these mythical animals from the lore of me-

dieval times would capture the interest of her students. Calder hoped that by working on the activities she designed for this theme, the children would become familiar with selected reference materials, learn to collaborate with peers *and* work more independently, reflect on life in a different era, read a selection of literature with a common theme, and acquire information from both fiction and nonfiction. The unit was to serve as the focus of almost all teaching and learning throughout the week. Figure 9 on the next page shows a web of the entire unit.

Calder began the work of putting together the unit by tracking down some books. She found a copy of Tomie dePaola's *The Knight and the Dragon* in a bookstore and was so charmed by it that she decided to use it as a springboard for the unit and for the week's read-in times. She proceeded to collect and borrow a number of books, fiction and nonfiction, about dragons and medieval times. Calder also found several dragon stories in children's magazines and in old collections of fairytales; these she stapled together between construction paper covers to create additional classroom reading materials. The books and stories were all identified with large blue stickers and set aside on a special table for the duration of the unit. Calder then made a word-to-picture matching game and a pocket chart version of dePaola's book. She copied Lilian Moore's "Dragon Smoke" (from *Poems Children Will Sit Still For*, compiled by de Regniers et al.) and "Leviathan" by Louis Untermeyer (from his *The Golden Treasury of Poetry*) onto chart paper and made tape recordings of both *The Knight*

117

Figure 9
An Overview of the Dragon Unit

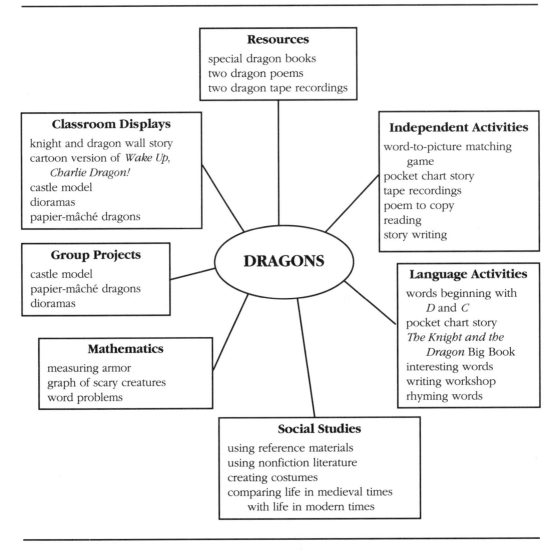

Resources
special dragon books
two dragon poems
two dragon tape recordings

Classroom Displays
knight and dragon wall story
cartoon version of *Wake Up,
    Charlie Dragon!*
castle model
dioramas
papier-mâché dragons

Independent Activities
word-to-picture matching
    game
pocket chart story
tape recordings
poem to copy
reading
story writing

DRAGONS

Group Projects
castle model
papier-mâché dragons
dioramas

Language Activities
words beginning with
    D and *C*
pocket chart story
*The Knight and the
    Dragon* Big Book
interesting words
writing workshop
rhyming words

Mathematics
measuring armor
graph of scary creatures
word problems

Social Studies
using reference materials
using nonfiction literature
creating costumes
comparing life in medieval times
    with life in modern times

and the Dragon and "Leviathan." She also asked the children to help her collect materials the class would need for the projects and activities by looking around at home for certain things.

Monday

For the first day's orientation, Calder began by holding up dePaola's *The Knight and the Dragon* and asking the children to predict the content of the story by looking at the cover. She wrote down four of their ideas on chart paper:

- I think the knight kills the dragon.
- No, the dragon kills the knight with smoke and fire.
- The dragon is really good. He helps the knight protect the castle from the bad guys.
- The knight trains the dragon and rides on him just like a horse.

She then read *The Knight and the Dragon* to the children, who thoroughly enjoyed the surprise ending. Afterwards Calder helped the children reread the predictions they had made. None had been particularly accurate, but she mounted the prediction chart on a bulletin board so the children could refer to these ideas later when they were writing their own stories.

Next Calder passed out the books she had collected and prepared for the unit. She explained to the children that some of the books might be difficult to read, but that the illustrations should have lots of interesting information. Reading time was usually a time for quiet work, but today the children were asked to share their discoveries about and from the books with their neighbors. After 25 minutes, Calder requested that the children close the special books and leave them on their desks.

Calder then asked the children what they knew about knights and dragons— their background knowledge always surprised her—and what they would like to know. On a piece of chart paper she jotted down seven questions they raised. Calder asked the children how they

might be able to find answers to these questions and how they could learn more about this theme. Several children pointed to books they had shared during reading time. Calder had borrowed three encyclopedia volumes from the school library and spent a few minutes giving a minilesson on what the children might expect to find in these reference books and how to locate topics listed in alphabetical order. One child looked up "Dragons," another found "Knights," and Calder searched for "Castles." The entries for those headings were shared with the class.

Some children worked alone and others worked in twos or threes to look over the encyclopedias and the other nonfiction books. Calder circulated among the children, reading passages from the more difficult books for them and responding to their excitement as they made new discoveries. Although this was a language activity, the skills of locating information in reference books would be useful for social studies, too.

Calder then called for everyone's attention for the beginning of sharing time. She read over each of the seven questions the children had raised earlier and asked if anyone had found any information about them. The children were able to answer three to their satisfaction. Calder suggested that they come back to the remaining four at the end of the week, after they had read more about these topics. She then asked those children who hadn't contributed very much if they had come across an interesting idea or picture they wanted to share.

The afternoons that week were dedicated to integrating the unit with other areas of the curriculum. To get things underway on Monday, Calder reread *The Knight and the Dragon*, this time asking the children to tell her what was happening in the illustrations. A child held the different pages open for all to see and Calder quickly wrote the children's descriptions on notebook paper (this was not a typical language experience exercise).

Then Calder gave each child a copy of a contract for the week (Figure 10). The children had worked with contracts before, and Calder had found them to be useful in a number of ways. They seemed to help the children assume responsibility for getting their work finished. (To avoid pressuring the children to tackle— or claim falsely to have completed—activities that were beyond their particular abilities, Calder made sure they knew they could go to their partners or to her for assistance. She always stressed that it was more important to do an activity well than to check off spaces on the contract.) Calder also found these contracts useful in keeping track of and evaluating children's work. The children brought their contracts to reading conferences so she could see the kinds of books they had been reading and could ask them appropriate questions. She was also able to monitor their responses to the different items on the contract and note their accomplishments. Today Calder read over the contract and explained the activities the class would be working on.

Next Calder helped the children read over the choices on the Things to Do chart and asked them if they had any questions about what they were to do in the different areas of the classroom.

Monday's chart listed the library, the special display table with books about dragons and knights, the word-to-picture matching game, and the listening center as places to explore and independent activities to undertake; Calder added other choices later in the week. She then told the class that they would be forming three groups and that each one would be involved in a different theme-related project. If at any time the children got stuck in their projects or finished their tasks, they could select from among the activities on the Things to Do chart and occupy themselves quietly until she could attend to them. She briefly described the three projects and the children selected the one that appealed to them most. The groups were fairly evenly divided.

Calder handed each of the children in the castle-making group a copy of the diagram that showed how to construct a model of a castle (Figure 11). She asked the children to look over the drawings and help each other read the directions. They were then to think of all the things they might need to create a castle fit for knights and ladies.

Group 2 would be working on dragons made from papier-mâché. Calder gave each child in this group a diagram of the "skeleton" of a dragon and guidelines for making a papier-mâché sculpture (Figure 12). She asked these children to read the directions as best they could, examine the diagrams, and decide how many dragons they wished to create. They could each make a small one, work with a friend to create one that was a bit bigger, or all work together to make one very large dragon.

Figure 10
Dragon Unit Contract

Name: _____ Date: _____

I finished the word-to-picture matching game. _____

I have read the pocket chart story and put the red cards in place. _____

The special project I worked on was _____ castle model

_____ papier-mâché dragon

_____ diorama

I have read these books:

_____

_____

_____

Here are some interesting words I found in the stories I read:

_____

_____

I listened to these tape recordings: _____ *The Knight and the Dragon*

_____ "Leviathan"

The name of the dragon story I wrote is

_____

_____

I have copied "Dragon Smoke" neatly. _____

I would like to know more about knights, ladies, castles, and dragons. This is my question:

_____

_____

After they had made their decisions, they could begin to tear newspaper into long strips. Calder gave them a large carton to hold the strips.

None of the children in Group 3 had heard of a diorama. By way of explanation, Calder showed them the materials they were going to use:

Figure 11
How to Make a Castle

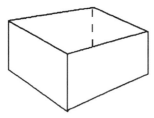

1. Cut the top off a cardboard carton.

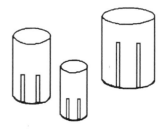

2. Cut notches along the top of the box.

3. Draw bricks or stones, doors, windows, and vines on the box.

4. Make 4 or 5 cylinder towers from thin cardboard. Cut 2 notches in bottom of each cylinder to fit over the box.

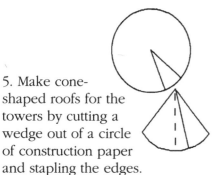

5. Make cone-shaped roofs for the towers by cutting a wedge out of a circle of construction paper and stapling the edges.

6. Attach the towers and the roofs and add a flag or two, a moat, and draw-bridge if you wish.

- shoeboxes (one for each child)
- salt-flour play dough
- construction paper
- pipe cleaners and popsicle sticks
- aluminum foil
- fabric, yarn, and cotton balls

- rubber bands
- crayons, paint, brushes, and glue

As they examined these materials, the children came up with all kinds of ideas for creating scenes. Calder asked them what kinds of things they might

Figure 12
Creating Papier-Mâché Dragons

1. Blow up 5 (or more) balloons and attach them together with some tape.

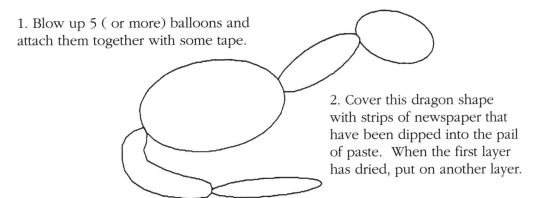

2. Cover this dragon shape with strips of newspaper that have been dipped into the pail of paste. When the first layer has dried, put on another layer.

3. When the layers of papier-mâché have dried, paint your dragon.

4. From construction paper cut out: two wings, two back legs, two smaller front legs, two ears, and a tail. Paste these onto your dragon.

5. Paint on two eyes, a mouth, some sharp teeth, toenails on the feet, and scales.

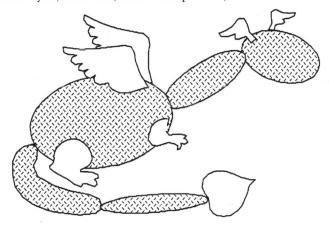

want to put in the foreground and what they might want to include on the paper that would cover the inside of the shoeboxes as background. She suggested that they do the background painting or drawing first and put this into place before they put in any of the foreground features. The children could create a medieval scene from their own imaginations or they could illustrate an aspect of *The Knight and the Dragon*.

Calder spent more than an hour moving from group to group, helping and consulting. First she brought out balloons, masking tape, and buckets of paste for the dragon makers. Two children had decided to create a small dragon and five were going to make something large—and very fierce! The castle makers had discussed the material they would need. Calder had already collected boxes of different sizes, heavy paper, string to hold the drawbridges, fabric and toothpicks (for the flags), foil (to simulate water in a moat), rulers, a stapler, markers, paint, and tape. She suggested that the children might want to decorate the castle's main walls before they attached the turret cylinders and showed them how to make conical shapes for the roofs.

These projects involved the integration of a number of subject areas. All of them involved an aesthetic response sparked by involvement with literature. The castle makers were required to use math skills to measure and build. The dioramas required planning and measuring. Rudimentary scientific thought was called for to adapt the two-dimensional dragons illustrated in books into three-dimensional sculptures. And all the children were using language skills to plan their work through various steps.

Clean-up took a little longer than usual. Calder showed the children areas in the classroom where each group could store projects and materials so they would be ready to use the next day. After everything was neatly put away, she asked the children to work in their journals. If they wished, they could write about the day's events. To end the day, Calder read the first three chapters of Marjorie Torrey's *Artie and the Princess*, a book she had picked up cheaply at a garage sale.

Tuesday

For Tuesday's read-in time orientation, Calder read the pocket chart version of *The Knight and the Dragon* to the children, pointing to each word as she went along. She then asked the children to join with her in a choral reading. She suggested that they might want to compare the original story with this version—she had condensed the text a bit since the original had too many words to fit easily in the pocket chart.

Calder then wrote the words "dragon" and "castle" at the top of a sheet of chart paper. She asked one child to read through the dePaola book and another to go through the pocket chart, searching for words beginning with *D* and *C*. At the same time, the rest of the children suggested other words that could be added to the lists, including *Calder, desk,* and *calendar.* Two *D* words and two *C* words were found in the book and pocket chart. After Calder wrote all the words on the chart, one child pointed to the words while everyone read along.

Most of the children kept two or three books from the classroom library in their desks to use during reading time. They took these out now while Calder passed out the books from the special collection. The children read quietly while Calder held four individual conferences.

Calder had decided that the children would create a class Big Book for the day's animating language activity. Using the text from *The Knight and the Dragon* and the children's descriptions of the illustrations noted the day before, Calder had written a 24-sentence version of the story. She had printed each sentence on a large piece of paper, ending up with

In addition to *The Knight and the Dragon*, Terry Calder found these books for the dragon unit:

The Story of Dragons and Other Monsters (Thomas Aylesworth)

A Dictionary of Fabulous Beasts (Richard Barber and Anne Riches)

The Incompetent Dragon (Janice Elliott)

The Lost and Found Princess (Jane Flory)

There's a Dragon in My Closet (John F. Green)

The King's Monster (Carolyn Haywood)

Ace Dragon, Ltd. (Russell Hoban)

Saint George and the Dragon (Margaret Hodges, adapter)

A Book Dragon (Donn Kushner)

Mystery Monsters of Loch Ness (Patricia Lauber)

Joji and the Dragon (Betty Jean Lifton)

Castle (David Macaulay)

Dragon Stew (Tom McGowen)

Paper Bag Princess (Robert N. Munsch)

Custard the Dragon (Ogden Nash)

The Book of Dragons (Edith Nesbit)

Wake Up, Charlie Dragon! (Brenda Smith)

The Popcorn Dragon (Jane Thayer)

Artie and the Princess (Marjorie Torrey)

Everyone Knows What a Dragon Looks Like (Jay Williams)

Monsters of the Middle Ages (William Wise)

one for each child. These sheets were numbered and mounted on a bulletin board.

Calder read the words on each page aloud, encouraging the children to read along and to visualize the kinds of illustrations that might be appropriate. The children volunteered to create illustrations for specific pages, and Calder wrote their names on the sheets where they would be visible once the illustrations were glued in place. She then passed out large squares of construction paper—blue for the outdoor scenes, tan for the castle interiors, and gray for the cave—along with chalk and crayons. Children who finished their drawings early helped with the covers and title page.

For sharing time today, Calder read each page again, pausing for a child to come up and glue his or her illustration just below the text on the appropriate page. She left the Big Book displayed on the bulletin board; at the end of the week she would bind it and place it in the class library.

The afternoon session began with a reading of one of the shorter stories about dragons from the special collection. Calder then used a cardboard mask to focus on certain words in the class Big Book of *The Knight and the Dragon*.

Now it was time for a quick math lesson. Calder had duplicated a rough outline of the human body and passed out a copy to each child. The children were to draw suits of armor on the outlines. They were then to work with a partner to measure each other, as if they were going to construct a suit of armor. The measurements (the length of an arm, for example) were to be printed on the outline to serve as a pattern for their own armor. Calder reminded them that when they finished they could work on their group projects and then select from the activities on the Things to Do chart. (The pocket chart story had been added to this list.) Calder also suggested that they check their contracts and work on some of the independent activities. Calder played a recording of madrigals on the phonograph while the class worked on the projects.

The children creating the dioramas were all proceeding independently and the dragons were receiving new layers of papier-mâché, but the castle makers were stuck. They had decided to collaborate on one very grand castle, but they were having difficulty agreeing on how it should appear and who should be responsible for what part. Calder listened to their frustrations and difficulties and together they arrived at a reasonable compromise that allowed the children to resume work. Toward the end of project time, several children filtered off to follow one of the suggestions on the Things to Do chart.

Calder wound up the day by asking the children once again to write in their journals. Several of them wrote about their projects and other aspects of the unit. Then Calder continued reading from *Artie and the Princess.*

Wednesday

Calder began the day by reading two more chapters from *Artie and the Princess*; the children then read *The Knight and the Dragon* Big Book chorally. On a piece of chart paper, Calder wrote the heading "Interesting Words We Have Come Across." She asked the children if there were any words in the Big Book that they had found interesting or unusual. They asked her to list *rum-*

maged, ancestors, armor, swishing, and *charging.* Calder suggested that they look for interesting new words whenever they were reading the special books and reminded them that their contracts had a place to write these words down. The children then read quietly for a time while Calder held six conferences.

Wednesday's animating language activity was a writing workshop. To focus their thoughts, Calder asked the children if they had any ideas for their own stories about dragons, knights, and ladies. Several children shared their thoughts. Calder referred the children to Monday's chart of predictions about *The Knight and the Dragon* for additional ideas. Then she made sure the children had everything they needed for writing and encouraged them to get started. While they wrote, she sat at the conference table and assisted different children who came to her to discuss their ideas.

At sharing time that morning several children wanted to read the beginnings of their stories to get feedback from their peers. Other children shared interesting pictures and bits of information they had come across during reading time.

In the afternoon, Calder first read another short book from the special collection and then brought out the two poems she had written on chart paper. She read each poem, encouraging the children to read along, and then they discussed briefly what the poems meant. She also referred to the contract and pointed out the line that suggested making a neat copy of "Dragon Smoke." She mounted the chart paper copy of that poem on the main chalkboard and a copy of "Leviathan" on a bulletin board in the listening center, where the children could listen to a tape of the poem and follow along with the text.

To start off the day's math lesson, Calder pointed out that dragons could be very scary and asked the children to think of other scary things, real and imaginary. She had prepared a rough eight-column bar graph in advance; when a child mentioned a frightening creature, she entered its name under one of the columns. Calder then distributed squares of paper and asked the children to draw a picture of their very scariest creature, label it, and staple it to the graph in the appropriate column. Comparisons were made and conclusions drawn about the most and least scary creatures.

Calder now asked the children how they were progressing on their group projects. She told them that she wanted all the work completed by Thursday afternoon, so the children would have time to share what they had been doing. She went over the choices on the Things to Do chart (which now included working on the dragon stories and copying out "Dragon Smoke") and reminded the children that they should try to complete some of the activities on their contracts.

When Calder circulated around the room during project time, she observed that several of the dioramas were finished. The papier-mâché dragons were dry enough to be painted and the children were cutting out wings, eyes, ears, teeth, and scales from construction paper to be glued onto the sculptures. And at last, the castle was recognizable: the basic structure was in place and the turrets and drawbridge were being added.

The children were also completing some of the activities on their contracts.

After clean-up, Calder went over the chart of interesting words. Six children suggested additions, and the whole class reread the entire list. Because they had engaged in a writing workshop earlier, Calder did not ask the children to write in their journals. Instead, she read aloud three more chapters of *Artie and the Princess*.

Thursday

Calder had fastened together the pages of *The Knight and the Dragon* Big Book and placed the book on an easel. She asked one child to pretend to be the teacher by turning the pages and pointing to the words. Calder sat with the rest of the children as they read their Big Book chorally. Two of them asked to reread the book alone and did so without assistance. Meanwhile, Calder wrote "knight" and "book" on top of some chart paper and asked the children to think of words that rhymed with them. Their lists were four and five words long. Calder and the children reread the words together and the chart was mounted on the wall. During reading time seven children came for conferences.

Calder read *Wake Up, Charlie Dragon!* by Brenda Smith to start the animating language session. This story from England tells about a dragon who sleeps until Guy Fawkes Day, when his friends awaken him to ignite their bonfire. Since most North American children are unfamiliar with this English holiday, Calder explained its history and told the children they would now make a "translation" of the story in a series of cartoons for the large bulletin board. She asked the children to name some holidays that were important to them. They discussed Thanksgiving, Halloween, Valentine's Day, and July 1 (Canada's national day) and decided to focus their cartoon on the last since celebrations of that holiday often include fireworks displays.

Then Calder divided up the labor. The children were to work in groups to create four images of every animal in the story (one for each cartoon panel). Three children were responsible for making four dragons—three identical sleeping ones and one that was awake and breathing fire on a firecracker. The children who finished early helped to make four trees and some fireworks. Calder circulated and asked the children what they thought their animals might say to wake Charlie up. She wrote down their words and drew balloons around them. The children then completed the cartoons by cutting out their word balloons and fastening these and their animals to sheets mounted on the bulletin board.

In sharing time that day, each group read the dialogue balloon for its own animal, and then they all read aloud the entire cartoon together. Calder suspected that the children would soon begin to use dialogue balloons in their independent drawing and writing.

After lunch, Calder reread the pocket chart version of *The Knight and the Dragon*, with some help from the children. Then she passed out 92 red word cards that duplicated the 92 black cards already positioned in the pocket chart. As she reread each word from the pocket chart, the child holding the corresponding red card came up and placed

it on top of the black card; soon the pocket chart changed from black to red. The subsequent choral reading received an enthusiastic response.

The day's math lesson focused on 12 word problems Calder had written on the chalkboard:

1. If a knight had 4 swords and 1 became blunt, how many would still be sharp enough to use?
2. If a knight made 3 lances and found 2 more, how many would he have for the big fight?
3. How many tails would 3 dragons have?
4. According to yesterday's graph, how many people in the class are afraid of snakes?
5. Are more people afraid of monsters or of bears?
6. If 3 people come into The Knight and Dragon Barbecue Restaurant and order hamburgers, how many will the dragon need to cook?
7. Suppose these 3 people want 2 hamburgers each. How many does the dragon have to fix now?
8. If each hamburger costs one dollar, how much money will the restaurant make?
9. Would a 20-foot-long dragon fit in this classroom?
10. Would a 10-meter-long dragon fit in this classroom?
11. How wide is the model castle at its widest point? How tall is the highest turret?
12. How long (from nose to tip of tail) is the small papier-mâché dragon? How long is the big one?

Calder read the first eight questions aloud and asked the children to figure out and jot down the answers independently; they could collaborate on solving the remaining four.

Project time was quiet this afternoon. Most of the children continued with their dragon stories, while several put the finishing touches on their castle. Calder talked with individual children about their stories and suggested that they work on the activities listed on the Things to Do chart when they finished.

Calder had reserved some time at the end of the day for the three groups to present their projects. The children explained in a fair amount of detail how they had made their creations, and Calder encouraged the audience to ask questions of the designers and builders. The children then added to their list of interesting words, and the day concluded with four chapters from *Artie and the Princess*.

Friday

Calder was curious to know what the children thought about *The Knight and the Dragon* and so she asked them what they liked or didn't like about the story. This led to a lively discussion about resolving arguments. Calder had the children recall what the knight and the dragon did instead of continuing their fight and then asked them what they did to settle disagreements before they became serious. As children shared their ideas for settling arguments, Calder wrote down several of them on chart paper (she thought these suggestions might be very useful someday!) and then she read over the completed list with the class.

During reading time later on, Calder met with the final five children for individual conferences.

The red cards were still in place in the pocket chart story when Calder distributed 22 picture cards tied to the story for the day's animating language activity. The children with cards described the illustrations, and Calder reread the story, pausing for different children to place their cards on top of the words they represented. The children then read the rebus pocket chart story to her. Next Calder asked if the children had fulfilled their contracts. Most of the children had not finished everything, and so they moved to various areas in the room to complete the independent activities during the remainder of language activity time. Those who had finished to the best of their abilities stayed in their seats to work on their dragon stories. By morning's end, seven children had stories, passages from longer books, or pictures they wished to share. Calder then read another two chapters of *Artie and the Princess*.

For the final afternoon of the unit, Calder wrote "In the Days of Knights and Ladies" and "Today" on the chalkboard. Then she posed these questions:

- Did children in the days of knights and ladies go to school? If so, what sorts of things did they learn? What sorts of things do children learn in school today?

- What were the homes of knights and ladies like? What are children's homes like today?

- What did knights and ladies do for fun? What do children do now?

Creating the materials needed for a theme unit—or for many activities associated with the shared book experience—can be time consuming. Assistance is available, however. Some schools hire teacher aides. Senior citizens are often eager to volunteer their services. If the school is near a university, student teachers can assist as part of their teacher training or as volunteers. Some high schools offer courses in childcare and parenting and might like the idea of their students receiving some hands-on experience.

Parents, of course, are the most obvious source of help. Many will be more than willing to donate materials; some may be available to assist in the classroom occasionally by reading with children, offering writing ideas, or supervising art projects. Parents can also help out in a more general way: by reading with their children at home.

This sort of involvement is particularly important if teachers are relying on the shared book experience approach. Most parents recall learning to read with basal readers and workbooks; newer whole language approaches may be difficult for many parents to understand and accept (Snyder, 1990). By seeking out parents' involvement, and by arranging open houses or even writing letters to parents explaining the philosophy and asking for their assistance, teachers will gain considerable support. This form of cooperation also relays to the child the important message that school should be a priority and that parents and schools can work together to foster successful learning (Fredericks & Rasinski, 1990, p. 521).

- What did they eat then, and what do you eat now?
- What did knights and ladies wear? What do you wear?

The children's knowledge surprised her: they were able to make numerous comparisons between the lives of medieval and modern children. Next the children turned their attention to the questions they had asked on Monday about knights, dragons, and castles. Some had already been discussed when the children were making their comparisons. The children contributed information they had gathered during the week and answered all but one question.

To end the unit with something special, Calder had collected materials for the children to create knight and lady costumes. Wearing their costumes, the boys and girls gathered around the author's chair to listen to several dragon stories by different children and then they did a dramatic reenactment of *The Knight and the Dragon*, using the large papier-mâché dragon as a prop. As a final celebration, the children "barbecued" marshmallows over a make-believe bonfire and enjoyed this treat with some fruit juice, while Calder finished reading *Artie and the Princess*.

Evaluating Children and Teacher

The many facets of the theme unit gave Calder ample opportunities to make informal assessments of her students' progress in a number of areas. Their attitudes toward and growth in reading were revealed by their participation in the read-in times and through individual conferences. Their contracts cast further light on these areas as well as indicating how well children were working independently. Just being able to finish the activities and complete the contract was quite an accomplishment for a first or second grader! Calder also compared the children's dragon stories with stories they had written earlier in the year and noted children's development in writing. The recopying of "Dragon Smoke" allowed her to assess improvement in penmanship.

When making her notes on each child's progress, Calder also took into consideration the children's enthusiasm for the theme and their willingness to explore different kinds of literature and reference materials. She observed how well they collaborated with their classmates on the projects and other activities. Finally, she noted the children's performance in the theme-related math and social studies activities.

Overall, Calder thought the theme unit had gone quite well. She had successfully integrated aspects of the prescribed math program with the unit and she felt that aims of the social studies curriculum had been well covered, although she admitted that she had not been able to think of ways to integrate activities in science. In addition, the children had had many opportunities to express themselves artistically. Music had been neglected (save for the playing of the madrigals), and Calder thought this should be remedied if she used the unit the following year. But in any theme there was bound to be a greater concentration in one area or another, and Calder realized that a balance could be achieved only with a variety of units.

Calder's most positive reflections focused on how easily literacy learning had complemented other areas of the curriculum. She was also pleased with the children's tremendous enthusiasm for the topic. They seemed eager to explore the different and often difficult reading and reference materials she had brought to class, and she was sure that many of them would continue to write and read about knights, ladies, castles, and dragons for many weeks to come.

The Pleasures of Learning

The flexibility of the shared book experience and its related activities makes it easy to incorporate children's literature into all aspects of the early childhood curriculum. Read-in time offers a way of managing this integration, whether it is an isolated and occasional part of the curriculum or the focus or one aspect of a theme unit.

With read-in time, children come to know what to expect. They receive direction and inspiration for reading in a group orientation, have an opportunity to explore books on their own, work together on activities related to their reading, and finally share their accomplishments and learn what others in the class have been doing. This familiar progression leads to a relaxed environment for learning. Read-in time also provides teachers with a routine that is structured but also flexible.

Through shared book experiences children hear many delightful stories, but each experience is more than a read-aloud session. The books that are shared provide the inspiration to turn pleasure into learning. Read-in time offers a way to manage and guide that learning as children discover the joys of books.

Predictable Literature and Other Resources

The shared book experience clearly relies on something other than a prepackaged set of materials. Instead, teachers must select predictable stories and other texts appropriate to the needs, interests, and degree of language development of the children in their classes.

Numerous predictable books have been mentioned in this volume, but there are certainly many more available. Because of their growing popularity and the fact that they are ideal for beginning readers, increasing numbers of these stories are published each year. In what follows I provide bibliographic information and brief descriptions of more than 100 predictable books, including all of those mentioned in earlier chapters. Although some of the older favorites may no longer be in print, teachers can ask the school or local librarian if they have or are able to get copies. Some, but not all, of these stories are available in Big Book format (many from Scholastic, Inc.); teachers may want to transform particularly the older publications into class-made Big Books for shared book experiences.

The appendix concludes with bibliographic listings of books containing stories from other lands and cultures, wordless books, and poetry collections and songbooks.

Predictable Books: An Annotated Bibliography

Aliki. (1968). *Hush little baby: A folk lullaby.* New York: Simon & Schuster.

The familiar song, in which Papa promises to buy his baby a number of things, makes a delightful predictable book. The accompanying illustrations are exquisite.

Barchas, Sara E. (1975). *I was walking down the road.* (Ill. by Jack Kent.) New York: Scholastic.

A young girl finds all kinds of interesting things as she walks around her neighborhood. This story is a good source of ideas for activities aimed at developing and at-risk readers.

Becker, John. (1985). *Seven little rabbits.* (Ill. by Barbara Cooney.) New York: Scholastic.

This is a charming verse about rabbits and numbers. The rabbits do have a definite objective in mind, but they have trouble following it. The illustrations are appealing; the verse is easy and repetitive.

Blair, Susan. (1963). *The three billy goats gruff.* New York: Scholastic.

Three goats seek a greener pasture—the one right beyond the bridge that belongs to a terrible troll. This version of the popular Swedish folktale is predictable and easy to read. It is a favorite for shared book experiences and prompts children of all levels to chant, "Trip, trap, trip, trap," and "Who's that tripping over my bridge?"

Bonne, Rose, & Garboff, Abner. (1961). *I know an old lady.* (Ill. by Abner Garboff.) New York: Scholastic.

A book version of the song about an old lady who swallows a fly, followed by a spider, a bird, a cat, a dog, a goat—and more. A delightful cumulative tale ideal for at-risk and developing readers.

Brown, Margaret Wise. (1954). *The friendly book.* (Ill. by Garth Williams.) Racine, WI: Western.

A perfect story for emergent readers that can lead to all kinds of individual and class writing activities. The illustrations are a delight.

Burningham, John. (1978). *Would you rather....* New York: HarperCollins.

What a series of choices Burningham presents! Would you rather have an elephant drinking all your bath water or a hippopotamus sleeping in your bed? This story can lead to many interesting extensions and variations. Developing and at-risk writers will be challenged to come up with all sorts of zany possibilities.

Burningham, John. (1983). *Come away from the water, Shirley.* New York: HarperCollins.

The family is spending a day at the beach. Father is giving Shirley all kinds of advice, but Shirley is off on a fantastic holiday of her own, complete with sailing ships, pirates, and buried treasure. At-risk readers will enjoy this imaginative story.

Burningham, John. (1983). *Mr. Gumpy's motor car.* New York: Puffin.

Mr. Gumpy takes his car for a spin. "May we come too?" ask his friends as they all pile in. When it starts to rain the car gets stuck and the friends, much to their displeasure, must get out to push. This is a terrific story for all readers.

Burningham, John. (1990). *Mr. Gumpy's outing.* New York: Henry Holt.

Mr. Gumpy decides to go out on his boat. First he is joined by two children, then a rabbit, a cat, a dog, a pig, a sheep, two chickens, a calf, and a goat. They all drift along happily for a while, but then things change....

Carle, Eric. (1973). *Have you seen my cat?* New York: Scholastic.

A boy travels the world looking for his missing cat. This book is predictable—with simple, repetitive language—but it has a surprise ending. It is ideal for emergent readers and can also be used with developing readers to promote writing activities.

Carle, Eric. (1977). *The grouchy ladybug.* New York: HarperCollins.

A grouchy ladybug wakes up and flies off to find breakfast. The ladybug sees a leaf with many tasty aphids, but another ladybug is there already. The ladybug goes on to encounter one fierce creature after another, but always manages to avoid a fight. After many close calls, the grouchy ladybug makes its way back to the original leaf and finds a few aphids left. Because of the number of words in this story, it is best suited to older readers.

Carle, Eric. (1981). *The very hungry caterpillar.* New York: Putnam.

One Sunday morning a caterpillar is born, and it goes on to eat its way through the seven days of the week—and the pages of the book! On the next Sunday, the caterpillar wraps itself in a cocoon, and two weeks later it emerges as a butterfly. This book is ideal for the very youngest readers.

Carle, Eric. (1984). *The mixed-up chameleon.* New York: HarperCollins.

The chameleon is most unhappy with his boring life. One day he visits the zoo and makes a wish that he could become a different animal. When his wish comes true, he wishes again and again until he is quite a strange-looking animal. And is he happy? Well, yes, when his last wish—to be himself again—comes true. This book has an important message for all readers.

Chance, E.B. (1970). *Just in time for the king's birthday.* New York: Scholastic.

A farmer makes an enormous cheese to give to the king on his birthday. He sets off to deliver it and encounters a number of inquisitive, hungry creatures. He lets each one have a sniff and a small bite of his magnificent cheese and comes to realize, too late, that the cheese is gone. The king happens by and is most understanding when he hears the farmer's story. All readers will enjoy this tale.

Chase, Edith Newlin, & Reid, Barbara. (1984). *The new baby calf.* New York: Scholastic.

Buttercup gives birth to a calf and nurtures him lovingly during his first days. The text is simple and predictable, making this book an excellent choice for beginning readers.

Chess, Victoria. (1979). *Alfred's alphabet walk.* New York: Greenwillow.

Alfred has been told to learn the alphabet, but he has other ideas. He takes off on his own, passing "ancient alligators," "brown bats," and "curious cats catching crabs." A highly amusing alphabet book perfect for emergent readers.

Cole, Joanna. (1986). *This is the place for me.* (Ill. by William Van Horn). New York: Scholastic.

A clumsy bear is tired of his broken-down house. He decides to move, but finding a new place is a little more difficult than he had anticipated. He finally finds a house that needs a few repairs—a house that looks strangely familiar! All children will enjoy this story.

dePaola, Tomie. (1980). *The knight and the dragon.* New York: Putnam.

The knight, a newcomer to battle, and the equally inexperienced dragon are intent on doing damage to each other. The time comes for the fight—and what a horrible fight it is! As both the dragon and the knight lie wounded, they have second thoughts about this business of battle. They welcome a young lady's suggestion that diverts their energies and talents to a completely new venture. Children love this charming story, much of which is told through the illustrations.

de Regniers, Beatrice Schenk. (1955). *What can you do with a shoe?* (Ill. by Maurice Sendak.) New York: HarperCollins.

A series of ridiculous rhymes about using everyday things in unusual ways. This book invites children to come up with some imaginative uses for objects in the classroom or at home.

de Regniers, Beatrice Schenk. (1989). *May I bring a friend?* New York: Macmillan.

This outlandish story is about a little boy who receives invitations each day to visit the king and queen. On each visit he brings along a different strange friend. The king and queen then accept an invitation for tea from the child. The tea takes place in a cage at the city zoo, and all the unusual friends are there. This is an ideal choice for emergent and developing readers.

de Regniers, Beatrice Schenk. (Reteller). (1990). *Red Riding Hood.* (Ill. by Edward Gorey.) New York: Macmillan.

This clever, humorous version of the familiar nursery tale presents the story in verse. The poem is simple enough for emergent readers, but the cunning approach also makes it suitable for developing and at-risk readers.

de Regniers, Beatrice Schenk, & Montresor, Beni. (1968). *Willy O'Dwyer jumped in the fire.* New York: Atheneum.

While trying to save a little girl, Willy O'Dwyer has a series of bizarre misadventures. The delightful verse is designed to captivate all readers and writers.

Domanska, Janina. (1969). *The turnip.* New York: Macmillan.

This cumulative story, based on a Russian folktale, has more and more animals and people join in to pull up a stubborn turnip. In this version, a magpie pulls on a pig's tail and sets off a chain reaction to unearth the vegetable. Domanska's illustrations are presented as a tapestry of cross-stitch and appliqué. This predictable tale is well suited to developing and at-risk readers.

Domanska, Janina. (1972). *I saw a ship a-sailing.* New York: Macmillan.

A series of delightful illustrations bring new life to this old rhyme. Four-and-twenty mouse sailors captained by an impressive duck are the crew for a ship that carries a most appealing cargo.

Domanska, Janina. (1975). *Din dan don: It's Christmas.* New York: Greenwillow.

This simple verse, based on a traditional Polish Christmas carol, tells of musical animals on their way to pay homage to the baby Jesus. The illustrations are as richly colored as stained-glass windows.

Domanska, Janina. (1977). *The best of the bargain.* New York: Greenwillow.

A clever hedgehog and a gullible fox are the characters in this adaptation of a Polish folktale. The two make a bargain to share the work and the harvest from the field and orchard, but year after year, the hedgehog outsmarts the fox. This clever story is especially appropriate for youngsters who are experiencing difficulty reading.

Domanska, Janina. (1987). *If all the seas were one sea.* New York: Macmillan.

What if all the seas were one sea and all the trees were one tree? The short text is accompanied by bold, colorful etchings that make this predictable book ideal for young children.

Eastman, P.D. (1960). *Are you my mother?* New York: Random House.

A bird hatches, falls from its nest, and begins the search for its mother by making inquiries of every animal and object it encounters. After an assortment of odd and potentially dangerous encounters, the young bird eventually succeeds. This story has long been a favorite among developing readers.

Elkin, Benjamin. (1957). *Six foolish fishermen.* (Ill. by Katherine Evans.) Chicago, IL: Childrens Press.

Before six brothers leave on a fishing excursion, one of them counts to make sure they are all there. He panics when he counts only five. Each of the brothers then counts, but each ends up with one brother missing. They begin searching for their poor missing brother when a boy comes along and helps them solve the mystery—each brother had forgotten to count himself. A super story for developing and at-risk readers.

Flack, Marjorie. (1971). *Ask Mr. Bear.* New York: Macmillan.

Danny does not know what to give his mother for her birthday. He asks a number of different animals for advice but none of their suggestions is quite right. Danny realizes that only Mr. Bear can help him, so off he goes alone into the woods. This story is just right for emergent and developing readers.

Fox, Mem. (1986). *Hattie and the fox.* (Ill. by Patricia Mullins.) New York: Bradbury.

Hattie the hen notices a suspicious creature hiding in the bushes. She tries to warn the other animals in the barnyard, but to no avail. The creature—a fox—emerges bit by bit. Finally Hattie realizes the extent of the danger and flies to safety while one of the other animals reacts very loudly. The fox flees and a cautious quiet returns to the barnyard. This is an ideal story for very young readers.

Gag, Wanda. (1928). *Millions of cats.* New York: Coward-McCann/Putnam.

A man and woman decide that a little kitten might make a nice addition to their home. The man goes off to look for a cat and finds not one but hundreds, thousands, millions of cats. The cats themselves manage to solve the problem of overpopulation. This classic, appropriate for all levels, has delighted children for generations.

Gelman, Rita Golden. (1985). *Cats and mice.* (Ill. by Eric Gurney.) New York: Scholastic.

The cats and mice are at it again—each trying to outdo the other. This book has many chapters, each a battle royal! The book is best suited for emergent readers because the words are simple and there is considerable repetition.

Ginsburg, Mirra. (1972). *The chick and the duckling.* (Ill. by José Aruego & Ariane Dewey.) New York: Macmillan.

A duckling hatches and greets the world enthusiastically; then a little chick is born. The chick is determined to keep up with the duckling and follows it everywhere. All goes along well until the duckling heads for the water. When the chick jumps in, too, the duckling must swim to its rescue. The chick and the duckling continue to be friends, but the chick comes to prefer dry land. This story, based on a Russian folktale, is well suited to very young readers.

Ginsburg, Mirra. (1987). *Mushrooms in the rain.* (Ill. by José Aruego & Ariane Dewey.) New York: Macmillan.

Rain begins to fall and an ant seeks shelter under a small mushroom. The rain continues and the ant is joined by a butterfly, a mouse, a bird, and even a rabbit—all under the same little mushroom. How they all fit is indeed a mystery! This adaptation of a Russian folktale is suitable for all children.

Greenberg, Polly. (1968). *Oh Lord, I wish I was a buzzard.* (Ill. by Aliki.) New York: Macmillan.

This story, appropriate for all readers, is about a little black girl who wishes she could fly around in the sky like a buzzard, curl up next to a rock like a snake, or dance from blossom to blossom like a butterfly—anything but pick cotton hour after hour under the hot sun. She looks forward to the end of the week and a treat she gets from her father.

Handy, Libby. (1982). *Boss for a week*. (Ill. by Jack Newnham.) Auckland, New Zealand: Ashton Scholastic.

There are lots of rules at Caroline's house, and she breaks every one! This is a story guaranteed to stimulate all kinds of ideas for discussion and writing activities. Although children at all levels can use this book, it holds special appeal for at-risk readers and writers.

Hoberman, Mary Ann. (1978). *A house is a house for me*. (Ill. by Betty Fraser.) New York: Scholastic.

This book explores all kinds of living quarters for all kinds of creatures and things. The illustrations are full of wonderful details. Although all children will appreciate the clever verse, it is especially suited to older children.

Hogrogian, Nonny. (1974). *One fine day*. New York: Macmillan.

In this Armenian folktale, a fox gets into considerable trouble when he upsets an old woman's pail of milk. The woman is so angry she chops off his tail. The fox is distraught and begs the woman to return his beautiful tail. She is willing, but only if he can get her another pail of milk. The fox begins his quest, but everyone

he asks for help has a request of his own. An excellent story for developing and at-risk readers.

Hogrogian, Nonny. (1974). *Rooster brother*. New York: Macmillan.

This Armenian folktale tells of a poor boy on his way home with supper who is accosted by three bandits who snatch away the evening meal. In a series of clever moves, the boy gets back at each bandit. Eventually he retrieves the supper and he and his mother feast heartily. This tale is in keeping with the interests of many older readers.

Hürllmann, Ruth. (1977). *The proud white cat*. (Trans. by Anthea Bell.) Worcester, UK: Kestrel Books, Trinity Press.

A proud cat is unable to find a suitable wife. He asks advice of Mrs. Vixen and they discuss all sorts of interesting possibilities: a moon, the sun, the mist, the wind, a tree, the rain, even a mouse. He finally realizes his foolishness and settles most happily on Katy Cat. This is a tale for developing and at-risk readers.

Hutchins, Pat. (1968). *Rosie's walk*. New York: Macmillan.

Rosie the hen decides to take a stroll through the farmyard. But she is not alone: she is being stalked by a hungry fox. In his attempt to snatch a tasty meal, the over-anxious fox meets with one calamity after another. In the final scene we see him dashing away, trying to escape from a swarm of angry bees. Rosie returns safely to her roost in time for dinner. This 37-word book has become a standard for shared book experiences.

Hutchins, Pat. (1972). *Good-night, owl!* New York: Macmillan.

Owls, readers soon learn, have habits that are quite different from other forest animals. The owl in this story is bothered incessantly by other creatures that share the same tree. But when day turns into night the owl gets its own back! This is a great book for emergent and developing readers.

Hutchins, Pat. (1976). *Don't forget the bacon!* New York: Greenwillow.

How carefully were you listening? Was it "six farm eggs" or "six fat legs"? "A cake for tea" or "a rake for leaves"? Hutchins thoroughly enjoys playing with words, as will all children who hear this irresistible tale.

Hutchins, Pat. (1986). *The doorbell rang.* New York: Greenwillow.

Mother has made cookies for Victoria and Sam, but the doorbell rings and guests begin to arrive. Pretty soon the house is full of friends and the plate of cookies is no longer enough. The doorbell rings again—but this time it's Grandma, just in time with a huge batch of cookies.

Hutchins, Pat. (1986). *The surprise party.* New York: Macmillan.

Have you ever played telephone? When a message is whispered around a circle from one person to the next, it often becomes muddled. That is what happens in this story—with amusing results. All ends well, however, and the party is quite a surprise. Ideal for emergent readers; older children will appreciate the humor, too.

Hutchinson, Veronica S. (1976). *Henny Penny.* (Ill. by Leonard B. Lubin.) Boston, MA: Little, Brown.

In this familiar story, an acorn falls on Henny Penny's head and she imagines that the sky is falling. This version is especially suitable for developing readers.

Kalan, Robert. (1989). *Jump, frog, jump!* (Ill. by Byron Barton.) New York: Morrow.

Poor Frog is in constant danger from all sorts of creatures that share its pond. Frog always manages to escape...but how? This cumulative story with interesting leaps is ideal for developing readers.

Keats, Ezra Jack. (1962). *The snowy day.* New York: Viking.

Peter awakens to find his world covered with snow. He hurries out to investigate and tries all sorts of experiments with the lovely white stuff—he even puts a snowball in his pocket to save for the next day. All readers will enjoy this story.

Keats, Ezra Jack. (1971). *Over in the meadow.* New York: Scholastic.

This text is an adaptation of an old children's rhyme. Animal mothers and their babies are seen in their natural habitat in the meadow. The rhythm and rhyme of this story appeal to a wide range of ages.

Kraus, Robert. (1971). *Leo the late bloomer.* (Ill. by José Aruego.) New York: HarperCollins.

Leo, a young tiger, is a little slow in his development. He can't read, draw, eat neatly, or even talk. His father is very worried about him, but his mother advises patience. After a year passes, Leo finally blooms. In his own good time he learns to eat neatly, read, write, and talk. This story is ideal for children who are experiencing difficulty reading.

Kraus, Robert. (1976). *Milton the early riser.* (Ill. by José Aruego.) Harmondsworth, UK: Puffin.

Milton is a delightful panda who likes to do strange things in the middle of the night. When dawn finally comes and the other animals awaken, Milton is just going to sleep. The text is simple and the illustrations are a joy. This story is a must for emergent readers.

Kraus, Robert. (1986). *Whose mouse are you?* (Ill. by José Aruego.) New York: Macmillan.

A young mouse is extremely sad: catastrophes keep befalling members of his family. The little mouse bravely rescues them one by one, and endears himself to them all. In the surprise ending, our hero discovers that he has a new family member. Emergent and developing readers will find much to love about this story.

Krauss, Ruth. (1989). *The carrot seed.* (Ill. by Crockett Johnson.) New York: HarperCollins.

A little boy plants a carrot seed. He is the only one who believes that it will grow. He waters it, he pulls away the weeds, and he watches and waits. One day a plant emerges, just as he knew it would. This simple text is just right for emergent readers.

Langstaff, John, & Rojankovsky, Feodor. (1955). *Frog went a-courtin'.* San Diego, CA: Harcourt Brace Jovanovich.

This story, based on an old song from Scotland, is about a frog and a mouse and the preparations for their wedding. All of the animals in the area join in the festivities and help prepare the wedding breakfast.

Langstaff, John, & Rojankovsky, Feodor. (1957). *Over in the meadow.* San Diego, CA: Harcourt Brace Jovanovich.

This book, a version of an old rhyme, is different from the Ezra Jack Keats book by the same name. The scene is a country meadow where the animals do whatever they do best. Along with the book, this version includes a phonograph recording of the text accompanied by music.

Lexau, Joan M. (Reteller). (1969). *Crocodile and Hen.* (Ill. by Joan Sandin.) New York: HarperCollins.

Hen wanders down by the river, looking for food. When she encounters a hungry crocodile, she calls him "Brother" and tells him he cannot eat her. Crocodile is completely mystified! "How can I be Hen's brother?" he asks, and seeks the advice of others. A clever story for all readers.

Lionni, Leo. (1960). *Inch by inch.* New York: Scholastic.

An inchworm would make a fine meal for a hungry robin, but it escapes by promising to measure the robin's tail. The busy inchworm is then called upon to measure a flamingo's neck, a toucan's beak, a heron's legs, a pheasant's tail, and a hummingbird's entire body. But what can it measure for the nightingale? Developing readers will be challenged to measure everything in sight.

Lionni, Leo. (1987). *The biggest house in the world*. New York: Knopf.

A snail is most unhappy with his size until his father tells him a story and he realizes that "some things are better small." This story within a story should intrigue developing and at-risk readers.

Lionni, Leo. (1987). *Swimmy*. New York: Knopf.

Swimmy is a curious little black fish who is fascinated by his world of lobsters, jellyfish, seaweed, anemones, and bigger fish—bigger, hungrier fish. Swimmy comes up with a scheme: he rounds up all his brothers and sisters and trains them to swim in a most unusual formation. An appropriate choice for developing readers.

Littledale, Freya. (1986). *The magic fish*. (Ill. by Ed Arno.) New York: Scholastic.

The theme of being granted three wishes appears in many folktales. In this one, a fisherman catches a magic fish who is really a prince in disguise. The fish asks the man to let him go and the man does so. The man's wife, appalled, demands that he recapture the fish and "make him give us a pretty house." The fish grants the wish, but is the wife happy? This is an excellent story for developing readers.

Lobel, Anita. (1975). *King Rooster, Queen Hen*. New York: Greenwillow.

A rooster and a hen are bored with life on the farm and decide to venture to the city to become king and queen. But they need so much: a carriage (an old shoe will do), some horses (field mice, of course), a maid (a volunteer sparrow), and so on. On their way they meet a fox and, for a moment, trust him. Soon they realize their foolishness and escape back to the safety of their farm. This longer, more involved plot is perfect for older readers.

Lobel, Anita. (1978). *The pancake*. New York: Greenwillow.

In this cumulative story, ideal for emergent readers, a pancake has visions of an adventurous lifestyle until he meets up with a hungry pig.

Lobel, Anita, & Lobel, Arnold. (1981). *On Market Street*. New York: Greenwillow.

A child goes shopping on Market Street to select a present or two for a friend. This charming verse, accompanied by beautiful illustrations, is in fact an alphabet book and offers children a terrific way to practice their letters.

Lobel, Arnold. (1977). *How the rooster saved the day*. New York: Greenwillow.

Every morning the rooster wakes up the sun to bring in the day. A robber plans to stop this practice by killing the rooster; he wants it to be dark all the time so his evil deeds will be hidden. But the rooster pretends to be deaf and tricks the robber into shouting cock-a-doodle-do loud enough to wake up the sun. This charming, witty tale is just right for developing and at-risk readers.

Lobel, Arnold. (1979). *A treeful of pigs.* (Ill. by Anita Lobel.) New York: Scholastic.

The farmer in this book is so lazy that he tricks his wife into doing all the farm work so he can sleep. Eventually she comes up with a trick of her own, and he promises from then on to do his share of the work. This story is suitable for all children.

Lobel, Arnold. (1984). *The rose in my garden.* (Ill. by Anita Lobel.) New York: Greenwillow.

The red rose is not alone in the garden; with each page of this book, other flowers and creatures join the group. This blissful scene is eventually disturbed by a cat on the prowl, and we are left again to admire only the lovely rose. All readers will enjoy this cumulative tale.

Martin, Bill, Jr. (1967). *Little princess goodnight.* (Ill. by Joseph Domjan.) New York: Henry Holt.

A fairytale princess and a unicorn, dragon, peacock, and mouse crawl into their respective sleeping places. But the mischievous mouse upsets the peaceful scene by pinching the peacock, who gets after the dragon, who attacks the unicorn, who starts to cry. The princess is very unhappy. She rearranges all of the creatures and they finally go to sleep. This delightful story is accompanied by beautiful woodcut illustrations.

Martin, Bill, Jr. (1967). *Ten little caterpillars.* (Ill. by Gilbert Riswold.) New York: Henry Holt.

The author turns ordinal numbers and a collection of caterpillars into a lovely poem. The illustrations are beautiful, but they may be appreciated more by adults than children.

Martin, Bill, Jr. (1970). *Brown bear, brown bear, what do you see?* (Ill. by Eric Carle.) New York: Henry Holt.

This very predictable story has become a standard read-aloud choice, especially appropriate for the youngest readers. The book is about large colorful animals that stare at other large colorful animals. Carle's delightful illustrations have become as familiar as the text.

Martin, Bill, Jr. (1970). *A spooky story.* (Ill. by Albert John Pucci.) New York: Henry Holt.

Out of the shadows comes the strangest assortment of scary creatures. They swirl around on dark pages and make weird noises. Although all children will enjoy this verse, it is ideally suited for emergent readers.

Mayer, Mercer. (1985). *Me too!* Racine, WI: Western.

A little sister wants to do everything her older brother is doing—which puts a real crimp in his style, although the last scene reveals a positive side to having a little sister. This story lends itself to discussions about families and caring.

Mayer, Mercer. (1987). *What do you do with a kangaroo?* New York: Scholastic.

The girl in this story has a series of incredible problems: a kangaroo complains about the sheets on her bed; an opossum isn't satisfied with the toothpaste she uses; a llama takes over her favorite pair of jeans; and a camel drinks her bath water. She tries to cope with all of these demanding creatures and settles for a compromise in the end. This amusing story is just right for beginning readers.

Mayer, Mercer. (1990). *There's a nightmare in my closet.* New York: Dial.

At bedtime the lights go out and things get scary. The boy in the story has his gun and cannon ready, just in case. One night he musters all his courage and opens the closet door. Sure enough, a monster emerges; only this nightmare is more frightened than the boy is and begins to cry when threatened with the gun. The boy and the monster end up sleeping peacefully together. This is a super story for emergent and developing readers.

McGovern, Ann. (1967). *Too much noise.* (Ill. by Simms Taback.) New York: Scholastic.

"I am going crazy," says Peter, an old man bothered by noise. He asks a wise man for advice and is given a very strange command: bring a cow into the house. This doesn't help, so the wise man tells Peter to bring a donkey into his house, and on and on through a series of other animals. When the situation becomes intolerably chaotic, the wise man tells Peter to let the animals go. Peace is restored and Peter is content with the relative quiet.

McGovern, Ann. (1986). *Stone soup.* (Ill. by Winslow Pinney Pels.) New York: Scholastic.

How can anyone make soup from a stone? A hungry young beggar can—at least he tricks an old woman into believing he can. Children enjoy the humor in this version of the popular folktale. It is best used in the classroom with older, at-risk readers.

McQueen, Lucinda. (1985). *The little red hen.* New York: Scholastic.

A little hen asks the other farm animals for help in planting wheat to make flour and bread. The animals all refuse until they see—and want to sample—the finished loaf of bread. The little hen has other ideas for her delicious bread, however.

Morris, William Barrett. (1970). *The longest journey in the world.* (Ill. by Betty Fraser.) New York: Henry Holt.

A little caterpillar spends the day crawling over high mountains, into deep valleys, around a huge castle, up steep walls, across wide rivers, and even past a sleeping dragon as he makes his way across a patch of garden. This book is full of gentle humor and delightful illustrations. Developing readers will especially enjoy this imaginative tale.

Mosel, Arlene. (Reteller). (1968). *Tikki Tikki Tembo.* (Ill. by Blair Lent.) New York: Henry Holt.

This hilarious tale, set in China, presents a plausible rationale for giving children short names. Children at all levels might want to come up with their own long names and their own variations to this tale. Beautiful pen-and-ink and wash illustrations accompany the story.

Preston, Edna Mitchell, & Bennett, Rainey. (1976). *The temper tantrum book.* New York: Puffin.

Why is the young lion having such a tantrum? Because his mother is combing his hair. And why is the baby elephant screaming? Because he has gotten soap in his eyes. It's hard to grow up when life presents so many obstacles. This story should strike familiar chords with all children.

Rose, Anne. (1976). *As right as right can be.* (Ill. by Arnold Lobel.) New York: Dial.

A delightfully whimsical story ideal for shared book experiences, especially with at-risk readers. A man's shoelace breaks and this sets off a chain of events and a series of purchases. Hidden within these comic events is a serious message about the importance of behaving responsibly.

Rossetti, Christina G. (1963). *What is pink?* (Ill. by Margaret A. Soucheck.) New York: Henry Holt.

This predictable story takes the form of a charming poem about colors and the world around us. A classic that will inspire children to come up with their own variations.

Schwartz, David M. (1987). *How much is a million?* (Ill. by Steven Kellogg.) New York: Scholastic.

How long would it take you to count from 1 to 1,000,000? How big would a goldfish bowl have to be to hold a million goldfish? This book gives answers to these questions and many more. Children experiencing difficulty in reading will be fascinated with this information about large amounts and huge sizes.

Sendak, Maurice. (1970). *In the night kitchen.* New York: HarperCollins.

Ah, alone at last! The parents are in bed and Mickey heads for the kitchen, where he encounters three bakers intent on baking a cake—with Mickey inside.... And this is only the beginning of a series of misadventures for Mickey.

Sendak, Maurice. (1987). *Chicken soup with rice.* New York: Scholastic.

Chicken soup makes an ideal meal every month of the year, or so this poem says. Younger children respond to the rhythm and rhyme, while older children use the basic structure and ideas to create adaptations of their own.

Sendak, Maurice. (1988). *Where the wild things are.* New York: HarperCollins.

What happens to Max when he is sent to his room without supper? He goes on a mad voyage and encounters the most fantastic assortment of monsters. With the words "Be still," Max tames these wild things and they all dance together by the light of the moon. Although the text is not particularly predictable, this story is such a favorite with children that it can readily be used in a shared book experience.

Seuss, Dr. (1957). *The cat in the hat.* New York: Random House.

It is too rainy to do anything but mope, but then a rather odd-looking cat comes to visit. This cat in the hat initiates a series of unbelievably mischievous deeds. All of Dr. Seuss's books are favorites of children, and because of their simple, rhyming language, they are ideally suited to the shared book experience.

Shulevitz, Uri. (1986). *One Monday morning*. New York: Macmillan.

A rainy day in the city...how depressing—unless you set your mind to wandering! The child in this story imagines that he is visited each day by members of the royal family and their entourage. A good book to use with emergent readers to focus on the days of the week.

Silverstein, Shel. (1964). *A giraffe and a half*. New York: HarperCollins.

A crazy, cumulative tale about a giraffe who encounters a series of animals and objects. Children who are experiencing difficulty in learning to read should find this poem particularly amusing.

Silverstein, Shel. (1983). *Who wants a cheap rhinoceros?* New York: Macmillan.

A ridiculous story about a boy and his most unusual pet, a very patient rhinoceros who consents to the oddest treatment. A book like this can lead children to imagine all sorts of uses for things, familiar or strange.

Slobodkina, Esphyr. (1947). *Caps for sale*. New York: HarperCollins.

A cap peddler has a unique way of presenting his wares—he stacks the caps, one on top of the other, on his head. One morning he is unable to sell any caps. Tired and discouraged, he settles down under a tree for a nap. He awakens to find a group of monkeys making off with his caps. How can he get them back? This classic is ideal for developing readers.

Smith, Brenda. (1986). *Wake up, Charlie Dragon!* (Ill. by Cherry Denman.) London: Hippo.

Charlie is an enormous, lovable creature who sleeps through all sorts of events. But the animals need Charlie because he can light their bonfire. This modern tale from England will need a little explanation for children across the Atlantic, but the charming storyline makes it worth the effort.

Spier, Peter. (1989). *The fox went out on a chilly night*. New York: Doubleday.

A traditional song about a fox on the prowl for food. He invades a barnyard and snatches a juicy duck for his family—and quite a feast they have! The detailed illustrations of a small hamlet and the countryside are perfect companions for the verse.

Supraner, Robyn. (1973). *Would you rather be a tiger?* (Ill. by Barbara Cooney.) Boston, MA: Houghton Mifflin.

Would you rather be a floppy puppy, a roly-poly piglet, a mischief-making monkey, or a child? This story encourages children to think about all the advantages of being just plain children and may lead to some ideas for writing activities.

Tarlton, John. (1986). *Have you ever seen?* Auckland, New Zealand: Ashton Scholastic.

Have you ever heard of a camel ice skating or a cat stamp-licking? Tarlton has created a series of hilarious animals engaged in the most absurd activities. At the end of the story the author/illustrator invites children to create additional silly sights. This challenge can be taken up by children at all levels.

Tarlton, John. (1987). *Going to Grandma's*. Auckland, New Zealand: Ashton Scholastic.

Visiting Grandma can be such an ordeal: there are so many things to do to get ready and so many things that can go wrong on the trip. This story will be appreciated by all children, but may be best suited to children having trouble with reading.

Tarlton, John. (1987). *The king's cat*. Auckland, New Zealand: Ashton Scholastic.

We all know how stubborn cats can be, but the king's cat wins the prize for willful disobedience. When the cat climbs a tree, the king has to ask for help from everyone in the kingdom to get the cat down. A small child gives the king some sound advice, and the cat comes down in its own good time.

Tolstoy, Alexei. (1968). *The great big enormous turnip*. (Ill. by Helen Oxenbury.) London: Heinemann.

"They pulled and pulled again, but they could not pull the turnip out of the ground." This familiar story is a simple and predictable version of a Russian folktale. An excellent choice for the shared book experience.

Tresselt, Alvin. (1964). *The mitten*. (Ill. by Yaroslava.) New York: Morrow.

A young boy drops his mitten in the forest, where a little mouse finds it and crawls inside to escape the cold. She is soon joined by a frog, an owl, a rabbit, a fox, a gray wolf, a wild boar, and a bear. A little cricket comes along and tries to crawl in, but the mitten can stretch no more. All children will enjoy this delightful adaptation of a Ukrainian folktale.

Ward, Leila. (1978). *I am eyes: Ni macho*. (Ill. by Nonny Hogrogian.) New York: Scholastic.

A young African child awakens one morning to the glorious sights all around. The text is simple and the theme is easily adapted to different settings.

Wells, Rosemary. (1973). *Noisy Nora*. New York: Dial.

Poor Nora is a middle child. Her simple requests are ignored; "Quiet!" and "Hush!" she is told, and she has to wait and wait some more. She finally gets fed up and leaves home, but she doesn't stray far. A delightful story about family life and love.

Wood, Audrey. (1985). *King Bidgood's in the bathtub*. San Diego, CA: Harcourt Brace Jovanovich.

This is a strange story, lavishly illustrated, of a king who is not very interested in being kingly—he would rather just sit in his bathtub. Various members of the royal court try to persuade him to get out of his bath; eventually a young page finds the solution. This story should appeal to older readers.

Zemach, Harve, & Zemach, Margot. (1989). *Mommy, buy me a china doll*. New York: Farrar, Straus & Giroux.

This story is based on a song from the Ozark region of the United States. Eliza Lou wants a china doll. She is willing to trade her father's featherbed and have him sleep in the stable. To the horse she offers her sister's bed; the sister can sleep in the baby's spot, and the baby in turn can be moved in with the kittens.... In the end Eliza Lou settles for a dream about a china doll. Older readers, especially those experiencing difficulty, should find this song/story very humorous.

Zemach, Margot. (1990). *It could always be worse.* New York: Farrar, Straus & Giroux.

The house is so crowded that everyone is always in everyone else's way. And what does the rabbi advise? Even more crowds and confusion. The rabbi knows when enough is enough and helps out one last time. This story is ideal for developing and at-risk readers.

Zolotow, Charlotte. (1987). *Some things go together.* (Ill. by Sylvie Selig.) New York: HarperCollins.

This poem develops a theme of love by describing perfect matches: music with dance and horses that prance; sand with sea and you with me. The book, with its beautiful illustrations, could inspire many individual and collaborative productions.

Anthologies, Poems, and Tales from around the World

Aesop. (1978). *The Caldecott Aesop.* (Ill. by Randolph Caldecott.) New York: Doubleday.

Arbuthnot, May Hill. (1961). *Time for true tales and almost true.* Glenview, IL: Scott, Foresman.

Asbjornsen, Peter C., & Moe, Jorden. (1969). *East of the sun and west of the moon: Twenty-one Norwegian folk tales.* (Ill. by Ingri d'Aulaire & Edgar Parin). New York: Viking.

Carle, Eric. (1980). *Twelve tales from Aesop.* New York: Philomel.

Chandler, Robert (Translator). (1980). *Russian folk tales.* (Ill. by Ivan Bilibin.) New York: Random House.

Childcraft How and Why Library. (1970). *Children everywhere: The 1970 childcraft annual.* Chicago, IL: Field Enterprises.

Clarkson, Atelia, & Cross, Gilbert B. (Compilers). (1980). *World folktales: A Scribner resource collection.* New York: Scribner's.

Cole, Joanna. (1983). *Best-loved folktales of the world.* New York: Doubleday.

Dolch, Edward. (1960). *Stories from Japan.* Champaign, IL: Garrard.

Hamilton, Virginia. (1985). *The people could fly: American black folktales.* New York: Knopf.

Haviland, Virginia. (1959). *Favorite tales told in England.* Boston, MA: Little, Brown.

Haviland, Virginia. (1972). *Fairy tale treasury.* (Ill. by Raymond Briggs.) New York: Coward-McCann.

Jones, Hettie. (Selector). (1971). *The trees stand shining: Poetry of North American Indians.* New York: Dial.

Lyons, Grant. (1972). *Tales people tell in Mexico.* New York: Julian Messner.

Manning-Sanders, Ruth. (1965). *The Hamish Hamilton book of magical beasts.* London: Hamish Hamilton.

Mitchell, Lucy Sprague. (1937). *Another here and now story book*. New York: Dutton.

Phelps, Ethel Johnston. (1983). *The maid of the North*. New York: Henry Holt.

Power, Effie. (1934). *Bag o'tales*. New York: Dutton.

Stontenberg, Adrien. (1966). *American tall tales*. New York: Viking.

Strickland, Dorothy S. (1982). *Listen children: An anthology of black literature*. New York: Bantam.

Summerfield, Geoffrey (Ed.). (1978). *Tales four*. London: Ward Lock.

Uchida, Yoshiko. (1980). *The sea of gold and other tales from Japan*. Boston, MA: Gregg.

Untermeyer, Louis. (1985). *The golden treasury of children's literature*. New York: Golden.

Wordless Books

Alexander, Martha. (1970). *Bobo's dream*. New York: Dial.

Carle, Eric. (1968). *1, 2, 3: To the zoo*. Cleveland, OH: World.

Carle, Eric. (1971). *Do you want to be my friend?* New York: Crowell.

Cristini, Ermanno, & Puricelli, Luigi. (1985). *In my garden*. Saxonville, MA: Picture Book Studio.

DeGroat, Diane. (1977). *Alligator's toothache*. New York: Crown.

dePaola, Tomie. (1978). *Pancakes for breakfast*. San Diego, CA: Harcourt Brace Jovanovich.

Goodall, John. (1977). *The surprise picnic*. New York: McElderry.

Hogrogian, Nonny. (1972). *Apples*. New York: Macmillan.

Keats, Ezra Jack. (1973). *Skates!* New York: Watts.

Knobler, Susan. (1974). *Tadpole and the frog*. New York: Harvey House.

Krahn, Fernando. (1974). *Flying saucers full of spaghetti*. New York: Dutton.

Krahn, Fernando. (1977). *The mystery of the giant's footprints*. New York: Dutton.

Lisowski, Gabriel. (1980). *The invitation*. New York: HarperCollins.

Mayer, Mercer. (1976). *Ah-choo!* New York: Dial.

Mayer, Mercer. (1977). *Oops*. New York. Dial.

Mayer, Mercer. (1977). *Frog goes to dinner*. New York: Dial.

Mayer, Mercer, & Mayer, Marianne. (1971). *A boy, a dog, a frog and a friend*. New York: Dial.

McCully, Emily Arnold. (1984). *Picnic*. New York: HarperCollins.

Ringi, Kjell. (1968). *The magic stick*. New York: HarperCollins.

Spier, Peter. (1981). *Noah's ark*. New York: Doubleday.

Wildsmith, Brian. (1970). *Circus*. New York: Watts.

Yolen, Jane. (1984). *Dragon's blood*. New York: Dell.

Poetry and Songbooks

de Regniers, Beatrice S., Moore, Eva, & White, Mary Michaels. (1969). *Poems children will sit still for: A selection for the primary grades*. New York: Scholastic.

de Regniers, Beatrice S., Moore, Eva, White, Mary Michaels, & Carr, J. (1989). *Sing a song of popcorn*. New York: Scholastic.

Hart, Jane. (1982). *Singing bee! A collection of children's favorite songs*. (Ill.

by Anita Lobel.) New York: Lothrop, Lee & Shepard.

Hogrogian, Nonny. (1972). *"One I love, two I love" and other loving Mother Goose rhymes.* New York: Dutton.

John, Timothy. (1978). *The great song book.* (Ill. by Tomi Ungerer.) New York: Doubleday.

Killion, Bette. (1983). *Poetry place anthology.* New York: Instructor.

Kuskin, Karla. (1980). *Dogs and dragons, trees and dreams.* New York: HarperCollins.

Lee, Dennis. (1975). *Alligator pie.* Boston, MA: Houghton Mifflin.

Lee, Dennis. (1983). *Jelly Belly.* (Ill. by Juan Wijngaard.) Toronto, Ont.: Macmillan.

Nye, Robert, Nye, Vernice, Aubin, Neva, & Kyme, George. (1970). *Singing with children* (2nd ed.). Belmont, CA: Wadsworth.

Prelutsky, Jack. (1966). *Lazy blackbird and other verses.* (Ill. by Arnold Lobel.) Toronto, Ont.: Macmillan.

Prelutsky, Jack. (1970). *The Queen of Eene.* New York: Greenwillow.

Prelutsky, Jack. (1976). *The snoop on the sidewalk.* New York: Greenwillow.

Rojankovsky, Feodor. (1942). *The tall book of Mother Goose.* New York: HarperCollins.

Untermeyer, Louis. (1959). *The golden treasury of poetry.* (Ill. by Joan Walsh Anglund). New York: Golden.

Worstell, Emma Vietor. (1961). *Jump the rope jingles.* (Ill. by Sheila Greenwald.) New York: Collier.

REFERENCES

Allen, R.V. (1976). *Language experiences in communication*. Boston, MA: Houghton Mifflin.

Allington, R.L. (1977). If they don't read much, how they ever gonna get good? *Journal of Reading, 21*(1), 57-61.

Anderson, R.C., Hiebert, E.H., Scott, J.A., & Wilkinson, I.A.G. (1985). *Becoming a nation of readers: The report of the Commission on Reading*. Washington, DC: National Institute of Reading, U.S. Department of Education.

Aukerman, R.C. (1971). *Approaches to beginning reading*. New York: Wiley.

Bader, L.A., Veatch, J., & Eldredge, J.L. (1987). Trade books or basal readers? *Reading Improvement, 24*(1), 62-67.

Bakst, K., & Essa, E.L. (1990). The writing table: Emergent writers and editors. *Childhood Education, 66*(3), 145-150.

Barr, R. (1975). How children are taught to read: Grouping and pacing. *School Review, 75*, 479-498.

Barr, R. (1982). Classroom instruction from a sociological perspective. *Journal of Reading Behavior, 14*, 375-389.

Berliner, D.C. (1981). Academic learning time and reading achievement. In J.T. Guthrie (Ed.), *Comprehension and teaching: Research reviews* (pp. 203-226). Newark, DE: International Reading Association.

Bishop, R.S. (1987). Extending multicultural understanding through children's books. In B.E. Cullinan (Ed.), *Children's literature in the reading program* (pp. 60-67). Newark, DE: International Reading Association.

Bloom, B.S. (1984, May). The search for methods of group instruction as effective as one-to-one tutoring. *Educational Leadership*, 4-17.

Bode, B.A. (1989). Dialogue journal writing. *The Reading Teacher, 42*(8), 568-571.

Bridge, C.A. (1979). Predictable materials for beginning readers. *Language Arts, 56*(5), 503-507.

Bridge, C.A., Winograd, P.N., & Haley, D. (1983). Using predictable materials vs. preprimers to teach beginning sight words. *The Reading Teacher, 36*(9), 884-891.

Bromley, K.D., & Jalongo, M.R. (1984). Song picture books and the language disabled child. *Teaching Exceptional Children, 16*, 114-119.

Burke, E.M. (1986). *Early childhood literature: For love of child and book*. Needham Heights, MA: Allyn & Bacon.

Calkins, L.M. (1983). *Lessons from a child: On the teaching and learning of writing*. Portsmouth, NH: Heinemann.

Calkins, L.M. (1986). *The art of teaching writing*. Portsmouth, NH: Heinemann.

Calkins, L.M., & Harwayne, S. (1987). *The writing workshop: A world of difference*. Portsmouth, NH: Heinemann.

Cazden, C.B. (1988). *Classroom discourse: The language of teaching and learning*. Portsmouth, NH: Heinemann.

Christie, J.F. (1990). Dramatic play: A context for meaningful engagements. *The Reading Teacher, 43*(8), 542-545.

Clark, M.M. (1976). *Young fluent readers: What can they teach us?* Portsmouth, NH: Heinemann.

Clay, M.M. (1979). *Reading: The patterning of complex behavior* (2nd ed.). Portsmouth, NH: Heinemann.

Cohen, P.A., & Kulik, J.A. (1981, December). Synthesis of research on the effects of tutoring. *Educational Leadership*, 227-229.

Coombs, M. (1987). Modeling the reading process with enlarged texts. *The Reading Teacher, 40*(4), 422-426.

Crouse, P., & Davey, M. (1989). Collaborative learning: Insights from our children. *Language Arts, 66*(7), 756-766.

Cullinan, B.E. (1987). Inviting readers to literature. In B.E. Cullinan (Ed.), *Children's literature in the reading program* (pp. 2-14). Newark, DE: International Reading Association.

Dillon, D. (1990). Editorial. *Language Arts, 67*(1), 7-9.

Doake, D. (1985). Reading-like behavior: Its role in learning to read. In A. Jaggar & M.T. Smith-Burke (Eds.), *Observing the language learner* (pp. 82-98). Newark, DE: International Reading Association.

Durkin, D. (1966). *Children who read early: Two longitudinal studies.* New York: Teachers College Press.

Durkin, D. (1974). A six-year study of children who learned to read in school at the age of four. *Reading Research Quarterly, 10*(1), 9-61.

Eliason, C.F., & Jenkins, L.T. (1986). *A practical guide to early childhood curriculum.* Columbus, OH: Merrill.

Estabrook, I.W. (1982). Talking about writing: Developing independent writers. *Language Arts, 59*(7), 696-703.

Fogarty, J.L., & Wang, M.C. (1982). An investigation of the cross-age peer tutoring process: Some implications for instructional design and motivation. *Elementary School Journal, 82*(5), 451-469.

Fountas, I.C, & Hannigan, I.L. (1989). Making sense of whole language: The pursuit of informed teaching. *Childhood Education, 65*(3), 133-137.

Fredericks, A.D., & Rasinski, T.V. (1990). Lending a (reading) hand. *The Reading Teacher, 43*(7), 520-521.

Gillespie, J.T., & Gilbert, C. (1985). *Best books for children* (3rd ed.). New York: Bowker.

Goodman, K. (1986) *What's whole in whole language?* Richmond Hill, Ont.: Scholastic.

Goodman, Y. (1987). Sing along with reading and writing. In D.J. Watson (Ed.), *Ideas and insights: Language arts in the elementary school* (pp. 96-98). Urbana, IL: National Council of Teachers of English.

Graves, D.H. (1983). *Writing: Teachers and children at work.* Portsmouth, NH: Heinemann.

Graves, D.H., & Hansen, J. (1983). The author's chair. *Language Arts, 60*(2), 176-183.

Gunderson, L. (1990). Reading and language development. In V. Froese (Ed.), *Whole-language: Practice and theory* (pp. 123-159). Scarborough, Ont.: Prentice Hall Canada.

Gunderson, L., & Shapiro, J. (1988). Whole language instruction: Writing in 1st grade. *The Reading Teacher, 41*(4), 430-437.

Guthrie, J.T., Martuza, V., & Seifert, M. (1979). Impacts of instructional time in reading. In L. Resnick & P. Weaver (Eds.), *Theory and practice of beginning reading* (pp. 153-178). Hillsdale, NJ: Erlbaum.

Hall, M.A. (1981). *Teaching reading as a language experience* (3rd ed.). Columbus, OH: Merrill.

Hall, M.A. (1986). Teaching and language centered programs. In D.R. Tovey & J.E. Kerber (Eds.), *Roles in literacy learning: A new perspective* (pp. 34-41). Newark, DE: International Reading Association.

Hall, N., & Duffy, R. (1987). Every child has a story to tell. *Language Arts, 64*(5), 523-529.

Hansen, J. (1987). *When writers read.* Portsmouth, NH: Heinemann.

Harste, J.C., Woodward, V.A., & Burke, C.L. (1984). *Language stories and literary lessons.* Portsmouth, NH: Heinemann.

Heald-Taylor, B.G. (1987a). Big books. In D.J. Watson (Ed.), *Ideas and insights: Language arts in the elementary school* (p. 85). Urbana, IL: National Council of Teachers of English.

Heald-Taylor, B.G. (1987b). How to use predictable books for K-2 language arts instruction. *The Reading Teacher, 40*(7), 656-661.

Hiebert, E.H. (1983). An examination of ability grouping for reading instruction. *Reading Research Quarterly, 18*(2), 231-255.

Hilliker, J. (1982). Labeling to beginning narrative: Four kindergarten children learn to write. In T. Newkirk & N. Atwell (Eds.), *Understanding writing: Ways of observing learning, and teaching* (pp. 13-22). Chelmsford, ME: Northeast Regional Exchange.

Holdaway, D. (1979). *The foundations of literacy.* Sydney, Australia: Ashton Scholastic.

Holdaway, D. (1982, Fall). Shared book experience: Teaching reading using favorite books. *Theory into Practice, 21*, 293-300.

Holdaway, D. (1984). *Stability and change in literacy learning.* Portsmouth, NH: Heinemann.

Holdaway, D. (1986). Guiding a natural process. In D.R. Tovey & J.E. Kerber (Eds.), *Roles in literacy learning: A new perspective* (pp. 42-51). Newark, DE: International Reading Association.

Holt, B.G., Ives, W., Levedi, B.L., & von Hippel, C.S. (1983). *Getting involved: Your child and science* (No. OHDS 83-31143). Washington, DC: U.S. Department of Health and Human Services.

Hubbard, R. (1986). Structure encourages independence in reading and writing. *The Reading Teacher, 40*(2), 180-185.

Huck, C.S., & Kerstetter, K.J. (1987). Developing readers. In B.E. Cullinan (Ed.), *Children's literature in the reading program* (pp. 30-40). Newark, DE: International Reading Association.

Hunter-Grundin, E. (1989, October/November). Learning centers in emergent literacy classrooms. *Reading Today, 7*(2), 28.

Jackson, N.E. (1988). Precocious reading ability: What does it mean? *Gifted Child Quarterly, 32*(1), 200-204.

Jalongo, M.R., & Zeigler, S. (1987). Writing in kindergarten and first grade. *Childhood Education, 64*(2), 97-104.

Katz, L. (1983). *Getting involved: Your child and math* (No. OHDS 83-31144). Washington, DC: U.S. Department of Health and Human Services.

Kintisch, L.S. (1986). Journal writing: Stages of development. *The Reading Teacher, 40*(2), 168-172.

Labbo, L.D., & Teale, W.H. (1990). Cross-age reading: A strategy for helping poor readers. *The Reading Teacher, 43*(6), 362-369.

Lamme, L.L. (1987). Children's literature: The natural way to learn to read. In B.E. Cullinan (Ed.), *Children's literature in the reading program* (pp. 41-57). Newark, DE: International Reading Association.

Manning, M., Manning, G., & Kamii, C. (1988). Early phonics instruction: Its effect on literacy development. *Young Children, 44*(1), 4-8.

Martinez, M.G., & Teale, W.H. (1987). The ins and outs of a kindergarten writing program. *The Reading Teacher, 40*(4), 444-451.

Martinez, M.G., & Teale, W.H. (1988). Reading in a kindergarten classroom library. *The Reading Teacher, 41*(6), 568-573.

Mass, L.N. (1982). Developing concepts of literacy in young children. *The Reading Teacher, 35*(6), 670-675.

Mavrogenes, N.A., & Galen, N.D. (1979, January). Cross-age tutoring: Why and how. *Journal of Reading*, 344-353.

Maxim, G. (1984). *The very young child: Guiding children from infancy through the early years* (2nd ed.). Belmont, CA: Wadsworth.

McClure, A.A. (1985). Predictable books: Another way to teach reading to learning disabled children. *Teaching Exceptional Children, 17,* 267-273.

McCracken, R., & McCracken, M. (1972). *Reading is only the tiger's tail: A language arts program.* San Rafael, CA: Leswing.

McCracken, R., & McCracken, M. (1978). Modeling is the key to sustained silent reading. *The Reading Teacher, 31*(4), 406-408.

McCracken, R., & McCracken, M. (1986). *Stories, songs, and poetry to teach reading and writing: Literacy through language.* Chicago, IL: American Library Association.

Nelson, O. (1989). Storytelling: Language experience for meaning making. *The Reading Teacher, 42*(6), 386-390.

Piazza, C.L., & Tomlinson, C.M. (1985). A concert of writers. *Language Arts, 62*(2), 150-158.

Pinsent, P. (1988). The implications of recent research into early reading. *Early Child Development and Care, 36,* 65-70.

Reutzel, D.R., & Fawson, P.C. (1989). Using a literature webbing strategy lesson with predictable books. *The Reading Teacher, 43*(3), 208-215.

Rhodes, L.K. (1981). I can read! Predictable books as resources for reading and writing instruction. *The Reading Teacher, 34*(5), 511-518.

Rosenshine, B.V., & Berliner, D.C. (1978). Academic engaged time. *British Journal of Teacher Education, 4*(1), 3-16.

Salinger, T. (1988). *Language arts and literacy for young children.* Columbus, OH: Merrill.

Sebesta, S.L. (1989). Literature across the curriculum. In J.W. Stewig & S.L. Sebesta (Eds.), *Using literature in the elementary classroom* (rev. ed., pp. 110-128). Urbana, IL: National Council of Teachers of English.

Slaughter, J.P. (1983). The graph examined. *Arithmetic Teacher, 30*(7), 41-45.

Slaughter, J.P. (1988). Classroom grouping and time-on-task in the whole language classroom. *Reading-Canada-Lecture, 6*(3), 149-155.

Smith, F. (1973). *Psycholinguistics and reading.* Orlando, FL: Holt, Rinehart & Winston.

Smith, F. (1978). *Understanding reading: A psycholinguistic analysis of reading and learning to read* (2nd ed.). Orlando, FL: Holt, Rinehart & Winston.

Smith, F. (1982). *Writing and the writer.* Orlando, FL: Holt, Rinehart & Winston.

Snow, C.E. (1983). Literacy and language: Relationships during the preschool years. *Harvard Educational Review, 53*(2), 165-189.

Snyder, G. (1990). Parents, teachers, children, and whole-language. In V. Froese (Ed.), *Whole-language: Practice and theory* (pp. 217-241). Scarborough, Ont.: Prentice Hall Canada.

Sowers, S. (1982). Six questions teachers ask about invented spelling. In T. Newkirk & N. Atwell (Eds.), *Understanding writing: Ways of observing, learning, and teaching* (pp. 47-54). Chelmsford, ME: Northeast Regional Exchange.

Spencer, M.M. (1986). Nourishing and sustaining reading. In D.R. Tovey & J.E. Kerber (Eds.), *Roles in literacy learning: A new perspective* (pp. 52-63). Newark, DE: International Reading Association.

Stewig, J.W., & Sebesta, S.L. (1989). *Using literature in the elementary classroom* (rev. ed.). Urbana, IL: National Council of Teachers of English.

Strickland, D.S., & Morrow, L.M. (1988). Creating a print-rich environment. *The Reading Teacher, 42*(2), 156-157.

Strickland, D.S., & Morrow, L.M. (Eds.). (1989). *Emerging literacy: Young children learn to read and write.* Newark, DE: International Reading Association.

Strickland, D.S., & Morrow, L.M. (1990). Integrating the emergent literacy curriculum with themes. *The Reading Teacher, 43*(8), 604-605.

Sulzby, E. (1985). Children's emergent reading of favorite story books. *Reading Research Quarterly, 20*(4), 458-481.

Taylor, W.L. (1953, Fall). Cloze procedure: A new tool for measuring readability. *Journalism Quarterly, 30*, 415-433.

Teale, W.H., & Martinez, M.G. (1988). Getting on the right road to reading: Bringing books and young children together in the classroom. *Young Children, 44*(1), 10-15.

Teale, W.H., & Sulzby, E. (1989). Emergent literacy: New perspectives. In D.S. Strickland & L.M. Morrow (Eds.), *Emerging literacy: Young children learn to read and write* (pp. 1-15). Newark, DE: International Reading Association.

Tompkins, G.E., & Hoskisson, K. (1991). *Language arts: Content and teaching strategies.* New York: Macmillan.

Tompkins, G.E., & Webeler, M.B. (1983). What will happen next? Using predictable books with young children. *The Reading Taecher, 36*(6), 498-502.

Torrey, J.W. (1979). Reading that comes naturally: The early reader. *Reading Research: Advances in Theory and Practice, 1*, 115-144.

Tovey, D.R. (1979). *Writing centers in the elementary school.* Bloomington, IN: Phi Delta Kappa Educational Foundation.

Trelease, J. (1989). Jim Trelease speaks on reading aloud to children. *The Reading Teacher, 43*(3), 200-206.

Vukelich, C. (1990). Where's the paper? Literacy during dramatic play. *Childhood Education, 66*(4), 205-209.

Wason-Ellam, L. (1988). Using literary patterns: Who's in control of the authorship? *Language Arts, 65*(3), 291-301.

Wells, G. (1986). *The meaning makers: Children learning language and using language to learn.* Portsmouth, NH: Heinemann.

Wyne, M.D., & Stuck, G. (1979). Time-on-task and reading performance in underachieving children. *Journal of Reading Behavior, 11*, 119-128.

AUTHOR INDEX

156

SUBJECT INDEX

Note: An "f" following a page number indicates that the reference is found in a figure.

157

BOARD GAMES: as beginning-reader resource, 40-41

BONNE, ROSE: 27, 83, 133

BOOK DRAGON, A (Kushner): 125

BOOKLETS, WRITING: 71

BOOK OF DRAGONS, THE (Nesbit): 125

BOOK REPORTS: 70

BOOKS: animal, 88-89f, 105, 109; dragon, 117-120, 125 (see also *Knight and the Dragon, The* [dePaola]); predictable (*see* Predictable books/literature/stories/text); wordless, 148. *See also* Accordion books; Basal readers; Big Books; Caption books; Minibooks; Predictable books/literature/stories/text; Print; Reading; Reference books; Shape books; Shared book experience; Stories; Writing

BOSS FOR A WEEK (Handy): 48, 138; brainstorming with, 65

BRAINSTORMING: prewriting activity of, 64; sentences derived from, 65

BRINGING THE RAIN TO KAPITI PLAIN (Aardema): 92

BROWN, MARGARET WISE: 72, 133

BROWN BEAR, BROWN BEAR, WHAT DO YOU SEE? (Martin): vi, 27, 72, 74, 142

BULLETIN BOARDS: 16, 23; Big Book supplementary materials displayed on, 28; rebus stories displayed on, 52; group illustrations displayed on, 48; picture cards displayed on, 30; writing samples displayed on, 68

BURNINGHAM, JOHN: 72, 75, 87, 88, 92, 133-134

CALDER, TERRY: 117-131

CAPITALIZATION: 17; language experience approach to, 28

CAPS FOR SALE (Slobodkina): 145

CAPTION BOOKS: 72

CAPTIONS: children's illustrations with, 48; child-written, 16; matching pictures and, 54

CARLE, ERIC: 8, 30, 32, 36, 56, 75, 85, 90, 134, 142; talent of, 80

CARROT SEED, THE (Krauss): 72, 88, 140

CARTOON: *Wake Up, Charlie Dragon!* as, 118f, 127-128

CASTLE: construction of, 118f, 120, 122f, 123-124, 126, 127, 129

CASTLE (Macaulay): 125

CAT IN THE HAT, THE (Seuss): 144

CATS AND MICE (Gelman): 137

CHALKBOARDS: 16; as beginning-reader resource, 4; as Big Board stand, 16; as brainstorming resource, 65; as language experience approach resource, 28; as picture-card mount, 30; visual cloze activities using, 51

CHANCE, E.B.: 42, 56, 72, 85, 134

CHARDIET, BERNICE: 92

CHART PAPER: Big Books created on, 18; flip stories on, 24; language experience stories on, 28; murals on, 110; poems on, 87; story scrolls on, 24; student comments displayed on, 28, 47-48

CHASE, EDITH NEWLIN: 33, 109, 135

CHEATING: collaboration as, 71. *See also* Copying

CHESS, VICTORIA: 135

CHICK AND THE DUCKLING, THE (Ginsburg): 27, 56, 90, 137; analysis of illustrations of, 31

CHICKEN SOUP WITH RICE (Sendak): 75, 85, 144

CHILDREN: collaboration of older/younger, 11

CHILDREN'S MAGAZINES: poetry in, 35

CHORAL READING: 24, 35-36, 47, 115, 124, 126, 127, 128

CLASS[ROOM] LIBRARY: 10, 96, 103, 106f; children's contributions to, 11, 19, 25, 44, 68, 75, 79, 84; as learning center, 99; location of, 101f; stocking of, 24; "user-friendly," 24

CLASSROOM(S): child-centeredness of, 66; layout of, 101f; teacher management of, 2

CLOZE ACTIVITIES: 39, 49-52, 95, 103, 106f, 116

COLE, JOANNA: 48, 74, 92, 135

COLLABORATIVE READING. *See* Choral reading; Groups; Partners, reading with

COLLABORATIVE WRITING: 71, 72, 74-75

COLLAGES: 79-82; book reviews as, 71; materials for, 81

COME AWAY FROM THE WATER, SHIRLEY (Burningham): 75, 87, 134

COMMUNICATION: 78; elements of (*see* Listening; Reading; Speaking; Writing)

COMPREHENSION, READING: 6; assessment of, 47; language experience approach to, 48; listening and, 9

COMPUTER: as Big Book-creation resource, 19; as writing resource, 73, 99

CONFERENCES, TEACHER/STUDENT: 10, 39-40, 55, 66, 67, 95, 96-98, 103, 105, 106f, 107, 109, 110, 112, 113, 115, 116, 120, 124, 126, 127, 129, 130; record logs for, 97-98; scheduling, 97; tables for, 101f

CONTEXT, SENTENCE: 49

CONTRACTS: classroom use of, 120, 121f, 126, 127, 129, 130

covers of, 29-32; animals in, 88, 89f; benefits of, 7-8; as Big Books, vi-vii, 2, 5-14, 133; as caption-book inspiration, 72; with chartable themes, 48; collaborative writing based on, 75; criteria for, vi; cross-curricular influence of, 78-93; described as such, vi; with family themes, 90-91; follow-up activities for, 39, 40, 45, 47, 49-56, 58-60; illustrations in, vi, 7; language experience approach and, 47-49; language patterns in, 8; mathematics incorporated in, 85; pocket chart stories as, 25-26; science-related, 87-88; song-based, 82, 83; story train derived from, 33; taping of, 51; typical, 27; vocabulary considerations with, 29; writing inspired by, 67, 72-74. *See also* Big Books; Shared book experience

PREDICTION(S): 6, 8, 9, 95; benefits of, 29; of Big Book story action, 29-32; of *Knight and the Dragon*, 118-119, 126; as learning device, 27; taping of, 31

PREFACE: Big Book, 21

PREPOSITIONAL PHRASES: in predictable stories, 29

PRESTON, EDNA MITCHELL: 143

PREWRITING: 64; brainstorming and, 65

PRINCE OF THE DOLOMITES, THE (dePaola): 92

PRINCIPAL, SCHOOL: as classroom guest, 76

PRINT: vi, 2, 95; comprehension of, 5, 6; mechanical aspects of interpreting, 6, 50; prereaders and, 3. *See also* Letters; Reading; Words

PRINT MAKING: 80, 82

PROJECTORS: Big Book illustrations made easier with, 21; filmstrip, 99; opaque, 21, 35; overhead, 5, 21, 23, 49 (*see also* Transparencies)

PROMPTS: story retelling and teacher, 42; during writing workshop, 67

PROUD WHITE CAT, THE (Hürllmann): 92, 138

PROVENSEN, ALICE: 109

PROVENSEN, MARTIN: 109

PUBLICATION: of student writing, 75-76, 98

PUBLIC LIBRARY: as resource, 24, 96

PUCCI, ALBERT JOHN: 142

PUNCTUATION: 17, 32, 56; errors in, 65; language experience approach to, 28; as minilesson topic, 66

PUPPETS: 100; construction of, 112-113; *Surprise Party*-based, 106f, 112-113, 114

QUESTIONS: for author/illustrator, 36; book-related, 32-35; classification of, 34; classroom use of,

128, 129-130; conference, 97; declarative sentences into, 55-56; math-related, 128-129; read-in time-related, 103-104, 109; shared book-related, 9; story extension-related, 45-47. *See also* Oral response; Prompts

RACKS: Big Book storage, 23

RAT IS DEAD AND ANT IS SAD (Baker): 92

READ-ALOUD SESSIONS. *See* Reading aloud; Shared book experience

READERS: remedial, 11. *See also* At-risk readers; Basal readers; Developing readers; Emergent readers

READERS THEATRE: 56

READING: 18; aloud (*see* Reading aloud); assessment of, 40, 103, 116; beginning, 1, 3-7 (*see also* Emergent readers); criteria for successful, 5-6; cross-age, 11; as curriculum unit, 8, 13, 77-93; difficulties with (*see* At-risk readers; Reading difficulties, books for children with); ensemble, 24, 35-36, 47, 115, 124, 126, 127, 128; independent, 39-41; IRA recommendations on, 12-13; as learning element, 11; mechanical aspects of, 6, 59; with partners, 10, 21, 22, 39-40, 47, 48, 49, 96, 99, 103, 105, 106f, 110, 113, 115, 119 (*see also* Reading, ensemble); practice essential to mastery of, 9-10, 39, 96; prekindergarten, vi, 3, 4; as prewriting activity, 64; programs for teaching, 5; shared (*see* Shared book experience); silent, 40-41, 96; teacher modeling of, 2; visual aspects of, 5; writing and, 61-76. *See also* Letters; Print; Reading aloud; Rereading; Shared book experience; Words

READING ALOUD: 95; benefits of, 4; by children, 40, 104; children's responses to, 6-7; discussion after, 75; ensemble (*see* Reading, ensemble); limitations of, 38; by parents, 3, 4, 5, 15 (*see also* Bedtime stories); as prewriting activity, 64; by teachers, 13 (*see also* Reading, teacher modeling of). *See also* Bedtime stories; Reading, ensemble; Shared book experience

READING DIFFICULTIES: books for chilren with, 140, 144, 145, 146, 147. *See also* At-risk readers

READ-IN TIME: 94-131; administration of, 106f; elements of, 95-103; evaluation of, 103-104. *See also* Theme units

REBUS STORY: illustrated cloze strip as, 52; pocket chart story into, 26, 55, 129

RECORDING(S). *See* Phonograph; Tape recording(s)